DA[illegible]SCH'S [illegible] PHOTOGRAPHY

COMPACT FIELD GUIDE

David D. Busch | Ed Verosky

Course Technology PTR

A part of Cengage Learning

COURSE TECHNOLOGY
CENGAGE Learning

Australia, Brazil, Japan, Korea, Mexico, Singapore, Spain, United Kingdom, United States

COURSE TECHNOLOGY
CENGAGE Learning

David Busch's Flash Photography Compact Field Guide
David D. Busch, Ed Verosky

Publisher and General Manager, Course Technology PTR
Stacy L. Hiquet

Associate Director of Marketing
Sarah Panella

Manager of Editorial Services
Heather Talbot

Senior Marketing Manager
Mark Hughes

Executive Editor
Kevin Harreld

Project Editor
Jenny Davidson

Series Technical Editor
Michael D. Sullivan

Interior Layout Tech
Bill Hartman

Cover Designer
Mike Tanamachi

Indexer
Katherine Stimson

Proofreader
Sara Gullion

For product information and technology assistance, contact us at **Cengage Learning Customer & Sales Support, 1-800-354-9706.**

For permission to use material from this text or product, submit all requests online at **cengage.com/permissions**. Further permissions questions can be e-mailed to **permissionrequest@cengage.com**.

Library of Congress Control Number: 2012934304

ISBN-13: 978-1-133-59716-2

ISBN-10: 1-133-59716-5

Cengage Learning is a leading provider of customized learning solutions with office locations around the globe, including Singapore, the United Kingdom, Australia, Mexico, Brazil, and Japan. Locate your local office at: **international.cengage.com/region**.

Cengage Learning products are represented in Canada by Nelson Education, Ltd.

For your lifelong learning solutions, visit **courseptr.com**.

Visit our corporate Web site at **cengage.com**.

Printed in the United States of America
1 2 3 4 5 6 7 14 13 12

Contents

Introduction

Throw away your cheat-sheets and command cards! Do you wish you had the most essential information you need to shoot compelling photos using your digital camera's built-in or add-on electronic flash? We've condensed the basic reference material you need in this handy, lay-flat book, *David Busch's Flash Photography Compact Field Guide.* In it, you'll find the explanations of *why* to use each of your camera's electronic flash features, and how to enhance your capabilities with the most versatile accessories. That's the kind of information that is missing from the cheat-sheets and the book packaged with your camera. Everything in this book is written to help you out in the field, as a quick reference you can refer to as you master the full range of things your digital camera can do in the flash realm.

About the Authors

Ed Verosky is an internationally renowned expert in flash photography as well as an accomplished editorial, wedding, and portrait photographer. As the author of several popular eBooks on photography, Ed has helped thousands of beginners, as well as professionals, gain a better understanding of difficult concepts through his unique style of teaching. Ed offers photography tutorials and advice through his websites and is a valued contributor on select internet-based forums and groups. He and his wife live and work in New York. Visit his website at edverosky.net.

With more than a million books in print, **David D. Busch** is the world's #1 selling digital camera guide author, and the originator of popular digital photography series like *David Busch's Pro Secrets, David Busch's Quick Snap Guides,* and *David Busch's Guides to Digital SLR Photography.* As a roving photojournalist for more than 20 years, he illustrated his books, magazine articles, and newspaper reports with award-winning images. Busch operated his own commercial studio, suffocated in formal dress while shooting weddings-for-hire, and shot sports for a daily newspaper and upstate New York college. His photos and articles have appeared in *Popular Photography & Imaging, Rangefinder, The Professional Photographer*, and hundreds of other publications. He's also reviewed dozens of digital cameras for *CNet* and *Computer Shopper*, and his advice has been featured on NPR's *All Tech Considered.* Visit his website at www.dslrguides.com/blog.

Chapter 1

Quick Start Guide

Although flash photography may seem challenging at first, it doesn't have to be. Today's digital cameras and compatible flash units are smart enough to make many of the hardest decisions for you. This chapter contains the essential information you need to get started with flash photography. You'll learn how to set up your flash unit and use automatic flash and camera settings to start taking great pictures right away. More advanced flash techniques are presented in subsequent chapters.

This *Compact Field Guide* has been written to help you get better flash photography pictures no matter what type of digital camera and dedicated external flash unit you have. The applicability of many of the features and techniques presented here however, is going to depend on your specific camera model and flash unit. If you have questions about whether or not a specific feature or option is available with your camera and flash combination, check your documentation. The basic manuals provided with your gear will also help you find certain settings and controls only available through menu navigation.

Setting Up Your Flash

To get the most out of your flash photography you'll have to make sure your camera and flash are equipped with sufficient power, are properly secured to the camera, and ready to go.

Batteries

Flash units consume a good amount of power and can drain batteries very quickly. Choose batteries based on how often you shoot, and the demands you expect to place on your flash. Most flash units use AA-sized batteries and some allow the use of optional external battery packs.

Of the AA-size, there are several types to choose from:

- **Alkaline.** One-use alkaline batteries are relatively inexpensive and adequate for casual snapshot photography. These are general-purpose batteries that perform well in moderate temperatures, but expect longer recycle times as they discharge from use.
- **Lithium.** Lithium batteries are more expensive than alkaline but last longer, providing you with more flashes. These batteries also weigh less than alkaline, perform well even in extreme temperatures, and provide consistent recycle times as they discharge. Be aware that lithium batteries can generate substantial heat during use and may not be recommended for use with some flash units.
- **Nickel-metal hydride (Ni-MH).** Rechargeable Ni-MH batteries offer great performance and value, especially if you go through several sets of batteries per year. As with lithium batteries, Ni-MH batteries offer a more consistent voltage over the discharge cycle than alkaline. Ni-MH batteries will begin to lose their charge even when not in use, so it's a good idea to recharge them regularly with a good Ni-MH battery charger (see Figure 1.1).

Whichever you choose, make sure you have more than enough fresh batteries on hand to get all the shots you want out of your flash. If practical, carry at

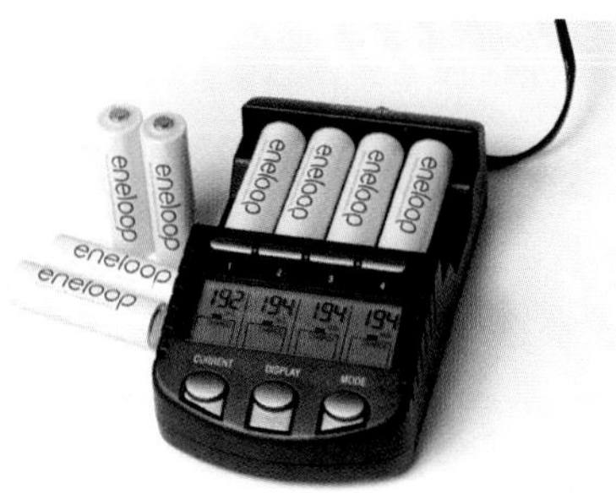

Figure 1.1 Rechargeable Ni-MH batteries and battery charger. Ni-MH batteries are recommended for their performance and cost savings over time.

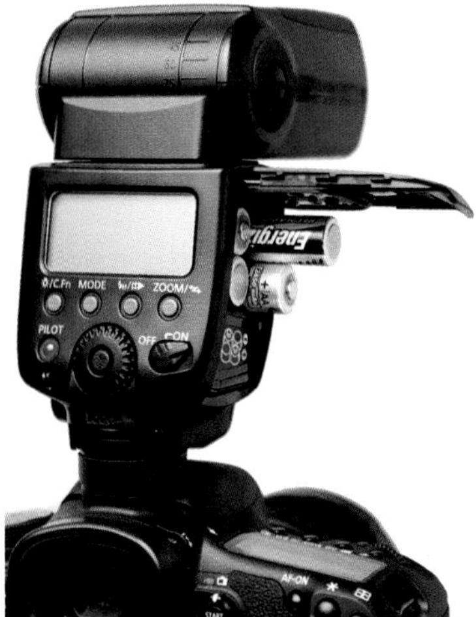

Figure 1.2 Batteries are inserted into the battery chamber.

least twice as many batteries as you think you'll need so you can focus more on your photography and less on battery power conservation.

Insert the batteries into your flash according to the instructions for your particular model (see Figure 1.2). Turn on the flash unit to make sure the batteries are providing adequate power. If your flash unit has a "flash ready" indicator light, it should come on immediately with a fresh set of batteries. If not, it could mean your batteries are not sufficiently charged. Some flash units will also make a distinct sound and/or display a "low battery" indicator icon on the LCD panel if the batteries are weak. If you get any of these indications of low battery power, replace the batteries with a fresh set. Turn off the flash unit when not in use.

Attaching and Securing the Flash to the Camera

If your camera is equipped with a built-in or pop-up flash, make sure it is off and closed so as not to interfere with the external flash. Follow these steps to attach your flash to the camera:

1. Make sure your camera and flash unit are both turned off.
2. Slide the flash unit's foot all the way into the camera's hot shoe, as shown in Figure 1.3.
3. Secure your flash unit to the hot shoe with the locking ring or lock lever mechanism particular to your flash model.

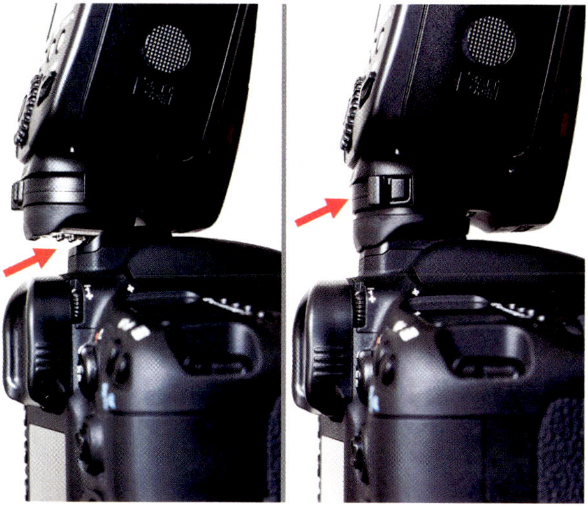

Figure 1.3
Slide the flash foot into the camera hot shoe (right). The locking mechanism should be set to secure the flash to the camera (left).

Attaching and securing your flash unit correctly not only ensures the flash remains on the camera during use but it will also help maintain the proper electronic contact alignment between flash and camera. The contacts are what allow your flash and camera to communicate the information necessary for basic and automatic flash output operations.

Adjusting the Flash Head to Normal Position

Check to see that the flash head is pointing straight ahead, in the same direction as your camera's lens (see Figure 1.4). Many flash units feature an adjustable flash head capable of tilting, and often rotating, off the normal lens axis. If you need to adjust the angle of your flash head, make sure you press the tilt/rotate release button if necessary. Forgetting to press the release button could damage your flash.

Some flash units have a subtle front-facing position that angles the flash head down just a few degrees from its standard forward position. This is for close-up flash photography and is not used for regular flash-to-subject distances. Check to make sure the flash head is not set in this position either by visual inspection of the flash head or by checking for the indicator icon for this position on the unit's LCD screen.

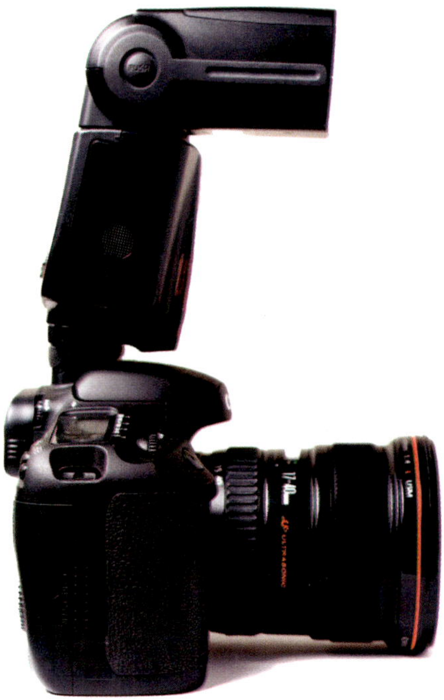

Figure 1.4
Normal flash head orientation. Be sure the flash head is not in the slightly lower, "close-up" position.

Using TTL for Automatic Flash Operation

Through-the-lens (TTL) flash metering is a technology that makes it easier than ever to get great pictures when using flash. With TTL, your camera and flash are able to work together to automatically determine flash output for each exposure. This is possible because, as the name implies, light from the flash is metered after passing through the lens where it can be instantly evaluated. This is most commonly accomplished via an almost imperceptible pre-flash which allows the camera to "preview" the flash exposure before taking the picture (see Figure 1.5). The information the camera gathers from this type of metering is used when sending a signal to the flash, controlling the output of light. This all happens automatically, and very quickly, often resulting in pleasing images.

Note

There are many implementations of this technology, including Nikon's i-TTL and Canon's E-TTL, but for the purposes of this *Compact Field Guide*, we'll be referring to it simply as TTL unless a more specific reference is required.

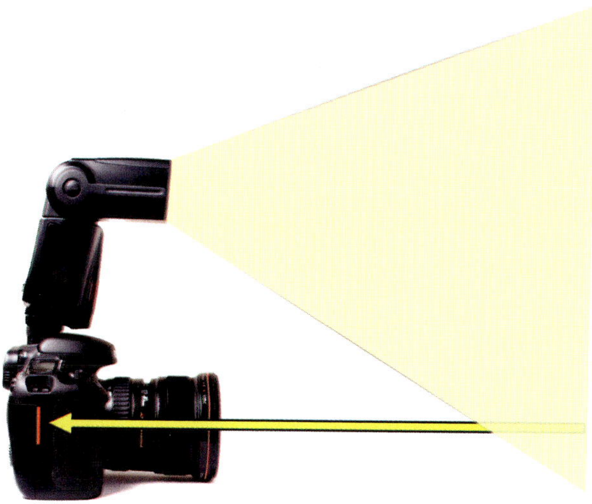

Figure 1.5
In TTL mode, an imperceptible pre-flash is measured as it reflects off the scene and back through the lens. The camera then calculates the correct flash output for the actual exposure.

Full Auto Exposure and Flash TTL Operation

The combination of your camera's automatic program modes and TTL for flash control makes it easier than ever to get great photos. Follow these steps to set up your camera and flash for this type of quick-and-easy flash photography:

1. Make sure the flash is properly attached to the camera and that both flash and camera are powered on.
2. Set your flash to TTL mode. This might appear as "TTL," "ETTL," or similar depending on your flash manufacturer and model (see Figure 1.6).
3. Set your camera to Full Auto mode (usually the green-colored mode on the mode dial). If your camera does not have a Full Auto mode, proceed to the next section for instructions on using Program (P) mode.

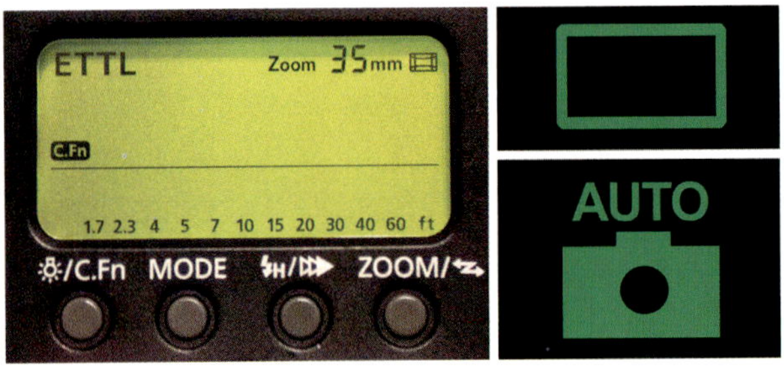

Figure 1.6 Flash in TTL mode (Canon ETTL). The camera's Full Auto mode is usually designated by a green-colored icon or square.

Now your flash and camera are ready for fully automatic flash operation. Simply compose your shots and depress the shutter button each time you want to take a flash picture.

Things you may notice when shooting are the AF-Assist beam, various sounds, indicator lights, blinking icons, and the sound of the flash recycling. These are things that you won't have to worry about most of the time, but will become accustomed to as you learn to use your flash.

Moving Past Full Auto for More Creative Control

Although you can get perfectly adequate exposures with your camera in Full Auto mode, coupled with your flash being in TTL mode, your creative choices are going to be limited. This is because the camera's Full Auto mode prevents you from making most, if not all, major decisions about things like ISO, shutter speed, f/stop, and exposure compensation.

Full Auto is the way to go when you want the best chance at getting properly exposed photos without having to think about any camera settings or make any major exposure decisions, but it's not foolproof. The camera will not always make the best decisions when it comes to exposure, and certainly not when it comes to more creative photography.

For those times when you'd like to have more creative control over your exposures, but you're happy to let the camera do most of the heavy lifting when it comes to keeping your settings in check, Program (P) mode is a good option. With your camera set to Program mode, and your flash set to TTL (see Figure 1.7), you'll be able to do important things like select the ISO and use Exposure Compensation (EC) and Flash Exposure Compensation (FEC). However, because Program mode is designed to keep things simple by managing some of your settings for you, it means there are limitations even to the settings you can adjust. Exposure Compensation, for example, is going to be limited somewhat by the camera's choice of shutter speed when the flash is attached. Many cameras prevent you from choosing a shutter speed higher than the maximum available with that camera and flash unit. They also may choose a slower shutter speed for special modes (such as Slow Sync), and, further, you may be able to select a range of shutter speeds that can be chosen in the camera's setup menus.

To use Program (P) mode together with TTL for flash control:

1. Make sure the flash is properly attached to the camera and that both flash and camera are powered on.
2. Set your flash to TTL mode. This might appear as "TTL," "ETTL," or similar, depending on your flash manufacturer and model.
3. Set your camera to Program (P) mode.
4. Set your camera's White Balance (WB) setting to Auto WB. See the "About White Balance and Flash Photography" section below.
5. Adjust the ISO to 400 or any setting of your choice. An ISO of 400 is a good starting point for most lighting situations, but you may find that a higher or lower setting is more suitable.

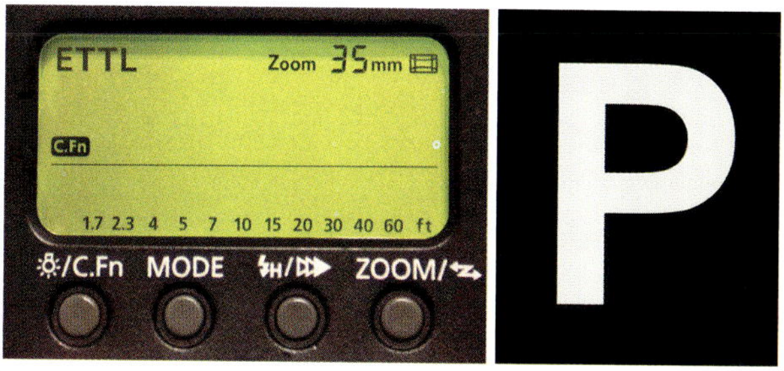

Figure 1.7
Flash in TTL mode (Canon ETTL). The camera's Program mode is usually designated by a capitol letter "P."

Your flash and camera are now ready for Program mode exposures and automatic flash operation. Simply compose your shots and depress the shutter button each time you want to take a flash picture.

Evaluating and Improving Your Shots

Digital photography offers us the ability to evaluate exposures instantly, so we can make on-the-spot adjustments to fix flash and lighting problems or improve our shots. Your camera's LCD monitor is your best on-camera tool for evaluating your exposures and helping you make adjustments. Besides simple previews of your images, the LCD monitor can display useful numerical and graphical data about an image. What that data means, and how to use it are what we'll show in this section. Accessing and presenting these types of data vary by manufacturer and often by camera model, so it's a good idea to learn how to access these views on your digital camera now, so you can use them quickly when needed.

Highlight Alert

Enabling the camera's highlight alert will warn you about overexposed areas in an image. The LCD will display your image as usual, but with an added "blinking" and/or color effect superimposed over areas in the image that have blown out any details, as shown in Figure 1.8. Because some very bright highlights are natural, and to be expected, this tool is most useful for warning you about areas of unwanted overexposure. If you're getting highlight alerts covering an area of detail in a white dress, for example, you'll want to dial down the flash exposure a bit on subsequent shots so the alert (and overexposure) disappears off the dress. That way, your camera will be able to record that detail sufficiently.

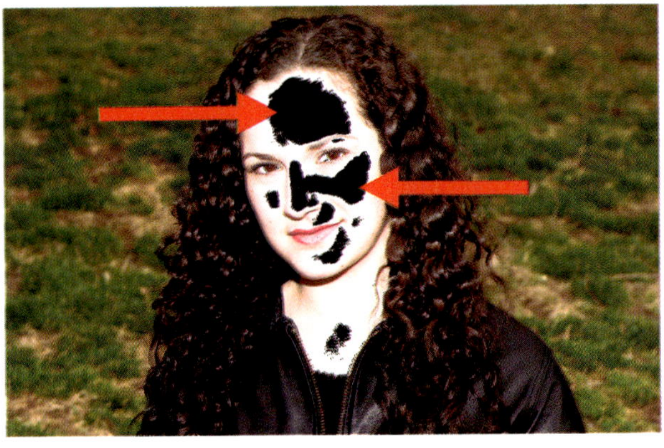

Figure 1.8
The red arrows point to the typical highlight alert/warning indicator. Blown-out highlights (areas which are so bright that they contain no detail) are indicated by blinking black areas.

Histogram

The histogram is a quick way to view the tonal values of an image your camera has recorded when other methods are not as precise. With the knowledge you'll get from this data, you can make quick, informed adjustments to your flash output and exposure settings if needed.

Your camera's histogram is essentially a little bar graph showing the distribution of tones in an image from darkest to brightest. The more pixels you have in an image making up a particular tone, the higher the bar appears for that tone. If most of the image is made up of very bright areas, the histogram will show more clusters of high bars on the right of the graph. If most of the image is made up of very dark areas, the histogram will show a heavier concentration of high bars on the left of the graph. A photo with a good tonal range (a good amount of darks, mediums, and brights) will show a relatively centered cluster of bars with some dark and bright areas represented, too.

With some cameras, the histogram also displays evenly spaced lines indicating five "zones" on the graph. These five zones correspond to the dynamic range of the sensor in your digital camera. The middle zone is where the medium tones are, while the zones to the left and right mark the one- or two-stops of difference (+/- 2 EV) in either direction (see Figure 1.9).

Having this graphical view of the distribution of all the tonal values can help you know what's going on with an image in ways that might not be obvious in the regular image preview. If you're shooting an image with a good range of medium tones (not too bright or too dark), the histogram would likely show

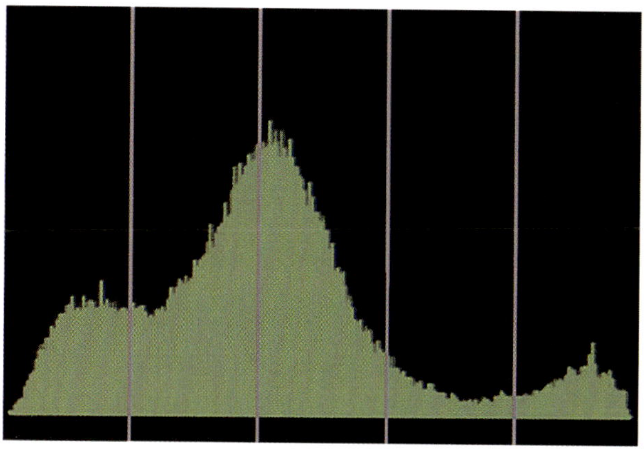

Figure 1.9
Five-zone histogram from an average scene. The green area is a bar chart detailing how many pixels are registered to each successive tone from darkest to brightest (from left to right) on the histogram.

the majority of the higher bars clustered and centered around the middle zone. If that cluster is actually falling more onto the next zone to the left, it would indicate that you might be underexposing the image by a stop or so. If it's falling more onto the next zone to the right, it might be overexposed by a stop or so. If this is the case, you might want to adjust your flash output and/or the camera's exposure settings.

LCD Monitor Preview

Use the LCD monitor preview (see Figure 1.10) to evaluate the overall image. Rather than serving up data or warnings, the standard preview offers a more subjective look at your image capture by helping you assess composition, the effect of lighting and shadow on the subject, and the look and feel of the photograph in general. The instant feedback provided by the previews gives you and your subject the opportunity to "fine-tune" the images to your liking. Posing and lighting changes can be made and evaluated on the spot until you and/or your subject are happy with the results.

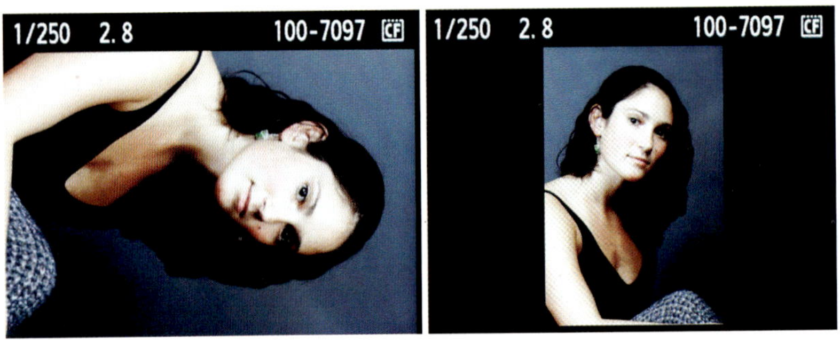

Figure 1.10 LCD monitor showing a visual preview of an image just taken. Images shot vertically can be rotated automatically or by the press of a button, which is useful when the camera is mounted on a tripod.

Flash Exposure Compensation (FEC)

Although every individual photo you take is considered a single exposure, in flash photography it's often useful to think of an image as being made up of two types of exposure: the overall exposure and the flash exposure. During the overall exposure, the camera records the effect of the constant light in the scene the same as it would if you were capturing an image without flash. An easy way to lighten or darken the scene is by dialing your camera's Exposure Compensation (EC) up or down. The part of the exposure most affected by the flash burst (which takes place for only a fraction of the total duration of the

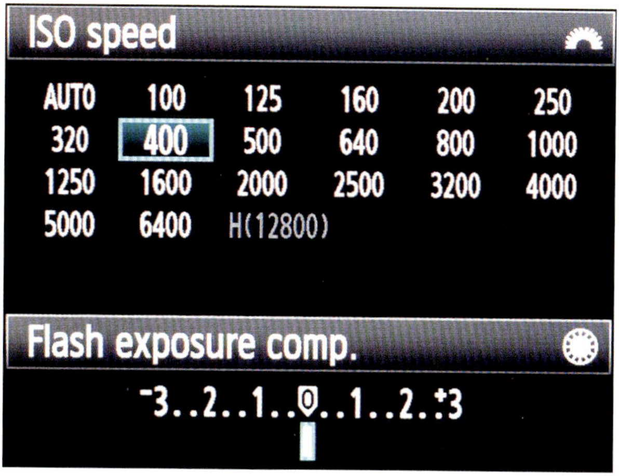

Figure 1.11
Flash Exposure Compensation scale on the LCD monitor, set to 0 (no compensation).

exposure) can likewise be adjusted through the use of Flash Exposure Compensation (FEC) (see Figure 1.11).

With some camera and flash systems, EC and FEC work independently of each other by default, while other systems couple these controls so that their effects are cumulative. Check your documentation for information on how these two controls affect each other where your camera and flash are concerned, and if there are ways to adjust the behavior. The ability to independently adjust EC (for background exposure) and FEC (for flash exposure of the subject) can be very useful.

Common Uses for FEC

Flash Exposure Compensation is useful under normal circumstances where slight to moderate adjustments to the flash output may be desired. As you can see in the following list, the use of FEC is straightforward.

- **Subject too dark.** If your subject is appearing too dark in the image, dial the FEC up to increase flash output.
- **Subject too light.** If your subject is appearing too light in the image, dial the FEC down to decrease flash output.
- **Fill light.** Outdoors, flash is most often used to add some extra light to your subject to help fill in shadows, soften contrast, and generally help them pop out a little from the background. Your digital camera and flash are probably able to work together to create fill light automatically. But if you're not getting exactly the look you want, subtle adjustments to FEC can help you achieve just the right amount of fill light. Note that outdoor shots may require the use of High-Speed Sync (see Chapter 2).

Proper White Balance and Flash Photography

White objects are almost always affected by natural and artificial color casts created by certain types of illumination and how that illumination is reflected off the environment. The casts, if left uncompensated for, will show up in your exposures, often making them appear too blue or too orange. The White Balance (WB) setting on your camera tells it how to deal with these color casts. When this setting is on Auto WB, the camera does its best to maintain a proper white balance but does not always succeed.

One way photographers talk about these color casts is by referring to the Kelvin scale which specifies a range of temperatures/degrees associated with the color spectrum. Colder colors are in the higher color temperature range, whereas warmer colors are in the lower range. For example, white daylight illumination and flash illumination are generally around 5,500K. Household lamps are closer to 3,200K (Figure 1.12).

Although color casts are always present, we don't tend to perceive them the same way our cameras will record them. We still think of a white dress, for example, as looking white, even if only illuminated by orange candle light. If we take a photo of the white dress in this scene, without any compensation for the overall color temperature, the photo will appear orange overall, including the dress.

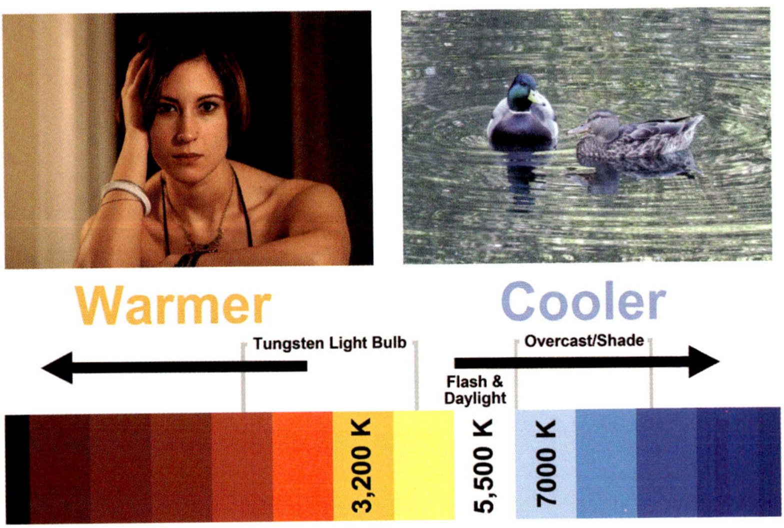

Figure 1.12 The top-left image was taken on Auto WB under tungsten lighting. The top-right image was taken on Auto WB under shade. The chart approximates the Kelvin color temperature scale.

The proper WB setting on your camera will help ensure that the white dress actually appears white in your photo, if that's what you intend. It does this by compensating for the orange when producing the JPEG, or alternatively, specifying the WB setting within the RAW file for correct color balance rendition by your RAW editing software. As stated before, when your camera is set for Auto WB, it will try to determine the proper WB setting for the scene. However, you can specify the WB setting yourself. For example, you can set the WB setting to tungsten when shooting in a mostly tungsten illuminated environment.

RAW FOR WHITE BALANCE

If you are capturing your images as RAW (or RAW+JPEG), you should know that the WB setting used when shooting an image is embedded along with other data in the RAW file. WB is not actually "burned-in" to the image at this point. This WB information is used to give your RAW file converter software an idea of the starting point for the WB settings for the image. Your RAW converter likely gives you the opportunity to dial in any WB setting you choose, after the fact.

If you are not working with a RAW file, but instead have exported a JPEG file out to your computer, the WB settings have already taken effect. You can still edit your JPEG with photo-editing software, but there isn't as much color data to work with as there would be with a RAW file. This means color corrections for WB are still possible at this point, but limited.

This is all fine when the color temperature of the light sources are all similar in a scene—a flash used together in bright daylight conditions (both types of light are about 5,500K). But what about when you're using flash (5,500K) in an environment of ambient household lighting (3,200K)? The WB cannot be set to compensate for both types of color casts at the same time, so a solution must be found.

Since this section deals with Quick Start tips, we recommend that you simply use Auto WB and let the camera determine the WB setting for you. This will generally result in good color rendition for outdoor shooting, and pleasing colors indoors, although there will be noticeable "warm" tones where background indoor illumination is a factor. That is because the WB setting will give the flash illumination a higher priority than the background illumination. In effect, this will ensure the flash lighting does not appear blue, which would be the case if the ambient tungsten were corrected to white.

As you'll see, in later sections, using a simple lighting gel, called a Color Temperature Orange (CTO) gel, along with a tungsten WB setting and possibly some RAW or JPEG color correction, will help resolve most issues when you're wanting to match your flash to interior ambient lighting.

Basic Flash Photography Tips

Here is a list of basic flash photography tips to get you started:

- **Know when to use flash.** Flash is a powerful photographic tool useful at times when additional illumination is necessary or desired. However, it's not always the best choice and won't always produce better photos. Sometimes the ambient or natural lighting in an environment is going to provide more pleasing light than your flash will. Don't use your flash just because it's there. Try switching from flash to natural light if you have the time and would like to compare results.
- **Stay within the flash distance range.** Your flash is capable of good exposures if used within the appropriate distance range. This range varies according to several factors including ISO sensitivity and aperture setting. If your flash features a distance range chart, it will show up on the unit's LCD monitor. Photos taken when the subject is within the displayed range should result in properly exposed flash images.
- **Take test shots.** Before you begin taking any important images, especially moments that you might not have another chance at capturing, be sure to take a test shot or two just prior. This will help you catch any problems with the flash or camera settings before it's too late.
- **Bounce the flash.** For indoor flash photography, tilt and/or rotate the flash head so that it points toward a light-colored surface (e.g., wall and/or ceiling) opposite the subject. This will help bounce the flash illumination around the room for softer, more pleasing light.
- **Avoid rapid-fire, continuous shooting.** A rapid succession of flash exposures will not only result in quick battery drainage, but may also damage your flash due to overheating. Some flash units are equipped with automatic shutoff switches to help prevent damage from overheating. Another reason to avoid this is because your flash might not be able to keep up the proper output during a burst of exposures, resulting in missed shots or underexposure.

- **Include ambient light.** Whether you're shooting indoors or outdoors allowing a little ambient (background) light to appear in your photos helps make them look more natural. This effect is automatically controlled for you in some shooting modes. It's generally accomplished with slower shutter speeds (e.g., 1/60 sec., 1/40 sec.) which allow more of the constant light from the environment to build up on the sensor during exposure, either before or after the flash has finished illuminating your subject.

Basic Flash Problems and Solutions

The following is a short list of problems you may encounter when using flash with your camera's Full Auto or Program modes. Depending on your camera model and flash, some of the solutions may not be possible in all modes.

- **Your subject appears too dark in the shot.** If the flash is too far from the subject, it can cause your subject to appear too dark in your images. No matter how powerful your flash is, its effectiveness decreases dramatically as the distance between it and your subject increases. Move your flash closer to the subject to correct this. Optionally, in some modes, you can use your flash's zoom feature which will increase the effective range of the output by focusing more of it into a narrower beam. This may, of course, result in some vignetting with wide-angle lenses since the flash's angle of coverage will be limited.
- **Your subject appears too light or washed out.** If the flash is too close to your subject, it can result in a washed-out or overexposed image. This can be a problem with some older, third-party, or low-end units. However, since many flash units can emit as little as 1/128 of their full power, overexposure is highly unlikely even at close distances. Another reason why this might occur is if your ISO is set too high. If you encounter this problem move farther from the subject and/or adjust your ISO to a lower setting. If your options with regard to distance and ISO are limited, you can try stopping down the aperture.
- **Light-colored background and/or clothing appears drab.** This is another situation where the image is actually somewhat underexposed, making light-colored objects appear darker than expected. The camera's TTL system assumes it is metering a scene of predominately mid-range tones and sets the exposure to reproduce that mid-range faithfully. Scenes with large areas of white or bright-colored surfaces can fool the metering system into thinking less light is needed for a proper exposure.

The result of this default metering behavior causes bright tones to reproduce as mid-tones, and mid-tones to reproduce as darker tones. Thus, if your subject is surrounded by a white wall, or wearing a white dress, she might appear too dark in the image, and the white may appear somewhat gray. If this is the case, a simple adjustment of flash output will solve the problem. This can be accomplished via Flash Exposure Compensation (FEC) adjustments.

- **Slow recycling times.** After a flash fires, it must pull enough power from the batteries to get ready for the next shot. If you're using fresh batteries and the shooting conditions aren't too taxing on the flash unit, the flash can recycle and achieve its ready state quickly between shots. If you notice, however, that it's taking longer and longer for the flash to recycle, you should change the batteries to avoid missing any shots while waiting for the flash to fully recycle.
- **Background is too dark (indoors).** The light from your flash reaches each area of the image with a different intensity. Closer objects (like your subject) receive more light from the flash than the objects and people farther away. In Full Automatic and Program modes, your camera and flash should automatically strike a good balance between background ambient illumination and the flash illumination on your subject. If you are not getting the results you want where ambient light in concerned, you may have to switch to a mode that allows for more control over the shutter speed (read more about this in Chapter 4). Slower shutter speeds will allow you to record more of the ambient light while maintaining the flash exposure on the subject.
- **Blue color cast.** If your WB setting is set to tungsten (often indicated with a "light bulb" icon), then any cooler light, including the light from your flash, will appear blue in the image. The tungsten setting tells the camera to compensate for the warmer colors of tungsten lighting so they look a little whiter/cooler. But that makes the cooler colors, like the white light from the flash, and or daylight appear too cool (blue). Indoors, either use a CTO gel to help match the flash output to the tungsten, or change the WB to Auto or Flash. Outdoors, simply changing the WB to Auto or Shade/Cloudy should do the trick.
- **Orange/Red color cast.** Indoors, if your WB setting is set to Flash, Shade, or Cloudy, and your flash output is very low, it can result in warm colors from tungsten lighting appearing too warm (orange/red). Make sure the WB is set to Auto or Tungsten to avoid this problem.

Chapter 2

Flash Features, Controls, and Modes

The use and availability of common flash features and controls vary by manufacturer and model. In this chapter, we cover several of the most common features found in many of today's mid- to high-end dedicated flash units. Refer to the documentation for your particular model if you need more information on how to use and access the controls and functions listed here.

It's important to note that many of the features on your flash are designed to work in conjunction with a compatible camera and its various modes, settings, lenses, and attachments. While it's possible to use third-party and non-dedicated flash units with most cameras, you'll likely get better results from a flash designed for use with your camera as part of the manufacturer's compatible "system" of products.

Standard Flash Unit Features

In this section, we'll provide an overview of several of the most common features found on typical mid- to high-end flash units. Your flash may not have all the features shown, such as the ability to swivel 180 degrees for bounce flash, autofocus assist capabilities, or all the optional exposure modes that the most sophisticated units have. However, most of the techniques in this book work with all but the most basic electronic flashes.

Features on the Front of the Flash Unit

Here is a list of the features commonly found on the front side of a flash unit:

- **Autofocus (AF) assist emitter/illuminator.** In low-light environments, the autofocus assist beam provides the illumination necessary for the camera and lens to achieve autofocus. This beam of light, emitted from a panel on the front of the flash, is usually red in color (see Figure 2.1).

- **Non-TTL metering sensor.** Older cameras often relied on the flash unit to meter and control its own output through the use of a built-in sensor on the flash. Some units still provide this Auto Flash functionality which does not require the use of TTL to get the job done. This type of flash metering is somewhat outdated and may not be available with your system.
- **Wireless flash sensor.** The use of wireless flash communication for TTL and multiple flash control require that each flash not only send control signals (usually via pulses of light), but also receive signals. Where light pulses are used, a small sensor on the flash unit can pick up the flash signals from other flashes and control devices.
- **Ready light indicator.** A ready light normally appears on the back of the flash unit facing the photographer. However, some units also display a ready light or other light indicators on the front of the flash. Some units use separate light emitters while others use the autofocus assist illuminator for this purpose. This is useful for remote flash operation to indicate when remote flash units are ready to fire.

Contacts and Connectors

Here is a list of the contacts and connectors commonly found on many flash units. Consult your unit's manual to see the exact location of these components on your unit:

- **Battery chamber.** This is where the batteries (usually AA-size) are inserted to power the flash unit.
- **Mounting foot.** The mounting foot features electronic contacts that match up to a dedicated camera when it slides into the camera's hot shoe. It can also be fitted to an off-camera adapter (TTL sync cord, non-TTL sync cord, or stand). Once the mounting foot is attached, it should be secured with its built-in mounting foot locking mechanism. It's important to engage the foot locking mechanism (often a tightening ring or lever). This will help secure your flash to the shoe.
- **Flash sync connector (often a PC terminal).** This is not standard on every flash unit and isn't compatible with TTL. PC terminals allow a flash to be triggered via a PC flash sync cord and are most often used with manual flash or with external auto metering on the flash unit. The other end of the sync cord is attached to the camera either directly or through an adapter that connects to the hot shoe.
- **External power connector.** External power packs, which hold more batteries than the flash's battery chamber, plug into the flash via the external power connector (see Figure 2.2).

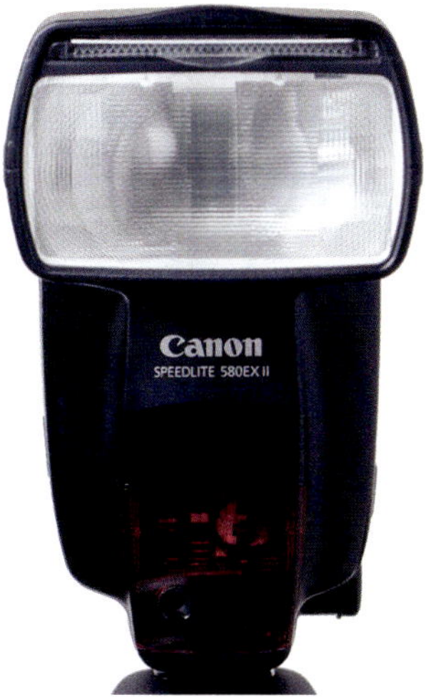

Figure 2.1 Electronic flash unit (front).

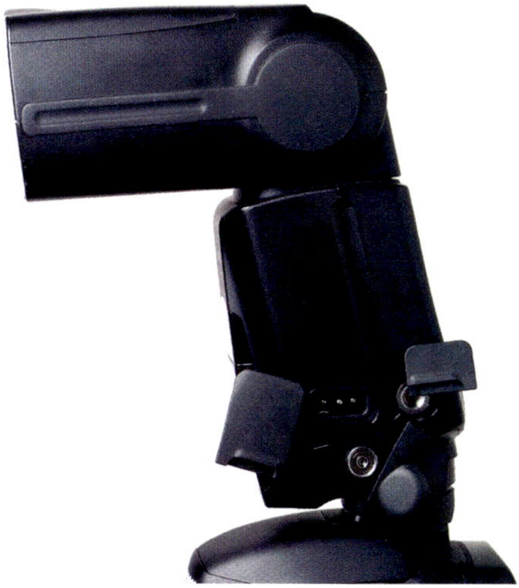

Figure 2.2 Electronic flash unit (side).

Flash Head

Here is a list of the features commonly found on the flash head:

- **Lens.** The front of the flash unit (see Figure 2.3) features a plastic face that protects the flash tube and, together with the zoom feature, modifies the way light from the tube is emitted from the front of the flash unit. Your flash may also feature a built-in or attachable wide-angle flash adapter to further modify the light output for use with certain lenses.
- **Bounce card.** Some flash units feature small, built-in bounce cards that can be used to create catch lights when using bounce flash. Catch lights are small specular highlights reflected in a subject's eyes, adding a little sparkle. Note this feature is different from the bounce card attachment discussed in Chapter 3.
- **Internal zoom.** Some flash units are equipped with a mechanical zoom feature that allows you to adjust the angle of the flash beam from wide to narrow. Flash zoom can be controlled manually or automatically and the amount of zoom is usually based on the lens attached to the camera.
- **Tilting/rotating lock release button.** Flash units with tilting and/or rotating heads have a lock that keeps the flash head in the position you set. The lock is released by pressing its corresponding button whenever you need to change the position of the head.

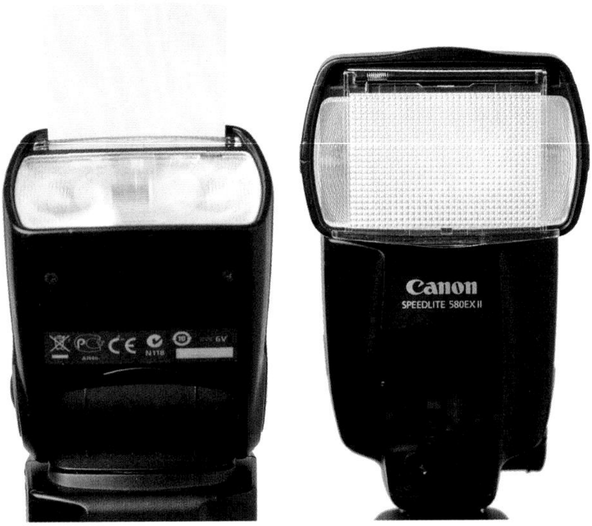

Figure 2.3
Electronic flash unit showing bounce card (left) and wide-angle adapter (right).

Features on the Rear Panel of the Flash Unit

The rear panel is where most of the flash unit's functions are controlled. Your flash unit may have buttons, switches, and dials that control everything from simple settings to menu navigation on the LCD panel, as shown in Figure 2.4.

- **Information/LCD panel.** The LCD panel provides you with a view of the flash's settings and menu navigation which are controlled by the buttons on the back of the flash unit.
- **Information/LCD panel illumination.** In low-light conditions, it may be difficult to see the information on the LCD panel of the flash without pressing this button, which provides backlit illumination for the LCD panel for a few seconds.
- **Mode selection.** Select various flash modes such as TTL, Manual, and Multi/Stroboscopic.
- **Master/remote selection.** A flash mounted on the camera for the purposes of controlling one or more off-camera flash units is assigned the role of "master." Any off-camera units being controlled by the master flash are set to "remote" or "slave."
- **Custom functions.** Many of the settings on your flash are less accessible from the main control panel because they're not changed frequently. See your flash's documentation for details on each of the custom functions available. These may include options for disabling the AF-assist, or changing the time your flash can be idle before turning off or going on standby.

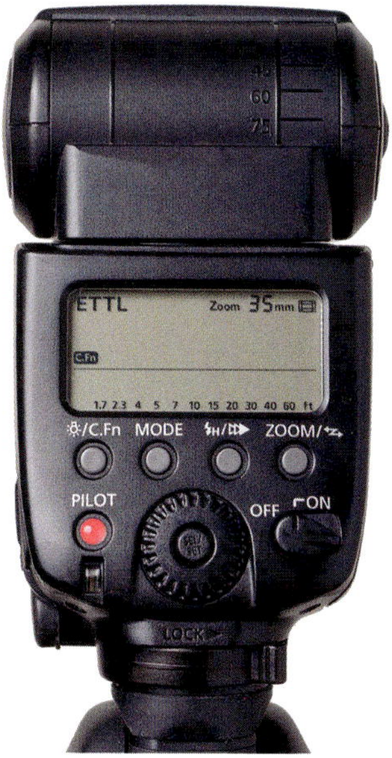

Figure 2.4
Electronic flash unit (back).

- **Ready light.** When the flash is fully recycled and ready to fire normally, the ready light indicator glows. Along with this, there may be status lights for near-ready "quick flash" and/or confirmation of standard exposure.
- **Test fire.** A test fire button allows you to fire the flash without depressing the shutter button on the camera. With multiple flash setups, the master unit can be test fired to check that the remote units are also firing as intended. The button is sometimes used to "wake up" a remote flash that has gone on standby mode.

Flash Modes Explained

Most flash units can operate in a variety of modes, including TTL, Manual, and Stroboscopic. These modes can be selected by pressing the appropriate buttons on the flash unit or set from the camera's menu if that option is available. Here is an explanation of what each of these modes is used for:

TTL Flash

Through-the-lens (TTL) flash metering makes it easy to get good flash exposures automatically. By combining your digital camera's automatic exposure modes with a compatible TTL-enabled flash (see Figure 2.5), most of the exposure decisions are handled for you automatically, allowing you to focus

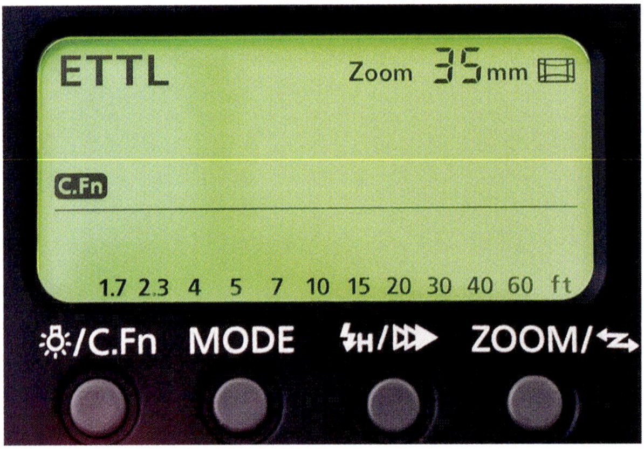

Figure 2.5
Flash LCD displaying TTL mode (Canon ETTL).

more on things like your subject and composition and less on flash output and distance calculations. TTL works by emitting a pre-flash and evaluating its effect on the scene just prior to exposing the image. The pre-flash is measured not by the flash itself, but by the camera after the light passes through the lens. The camera instantaneously determines what the flash output should be for the actual exposure and sends that information to the flash. (See Chapter 1 for more on setting up and using TTL.) TTL flash can also be used with the camera's Manual mode.

Manual Flash

Manual flash control works independently of any metering and automatic controls, allowing you to set a specific flash output power. While not generally as quick and easy to use as TTL, it does offer some advantages where creative control is desired. Specifically, Manual flash (see Figure 2.6) is suited to portraiture and other subjects where most of the scene, as well as the distance from flash to subject, remains rather constant. In off-camera applications, this allows the photographer to vary his distance from the subject without causing changes to flash exposure, because the distance from subject to flash unit(s) remains the same.

Stroboscopic and Other Flash Modes

Stroboscopic (multi/repeating) flash (see Figure 2.7) is a special-effect mode which creates multiple flash exposures within a single shot. The flash fires repeatedly during longer exposures in order to capture a subject in different positions within the frame. See your flash documentation for specific instructions on using this feature.

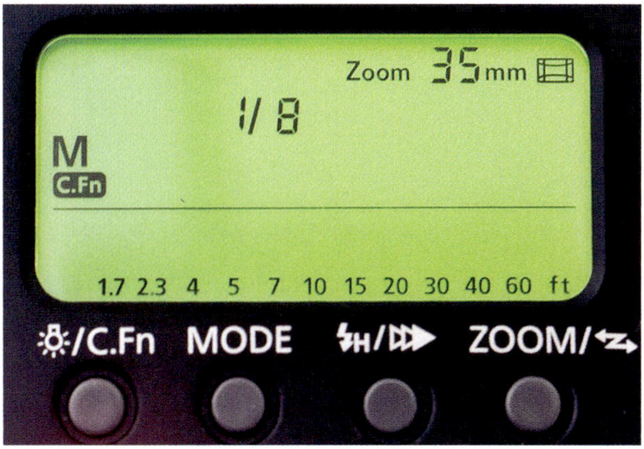

Figure 2.6
Flash LCD displaying Manual mode with power set to 1/8.

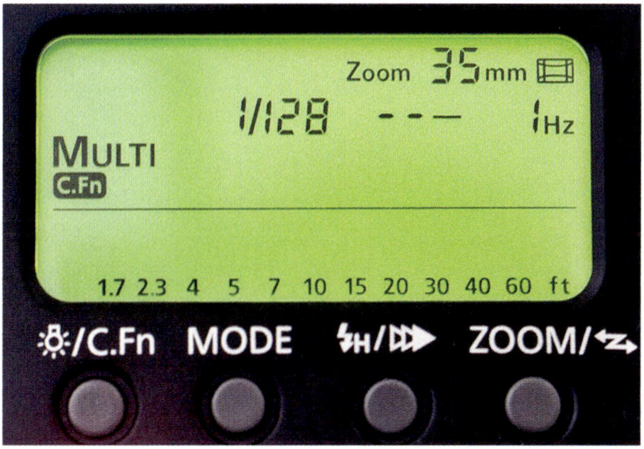

Figure 2.7
Flash LCD displaying Stroboscopic mode (Canon Multi).

Other modes available depending on manufacturer or flash model generally fall in the category of non-TTL automatic external metering. A metering sensor located on the flash unit measures the light and controls output independently of the camera. If available, modes like Auto External Metering, Manual External Metering, and Auto Flash, can be set from your flash's main control panel and/or custom features menu. These modes are not applicable to this *Compact Field Guide*, so they will not be covered.

Main Functions and Settings

Some of the following functions and settings are available at the touch of a single button or combination of buttons. Some are set automatically when you change other settings. Menu navigation, on the camera or flash unit, is required to get to many of the options available. The main functions and settings we'll cover are:

- High-Speed (FP) Flash Sync
- Front/Rear Curtain Sync
- Flash Exposure Compensation (FEC)
- Flash Zoom
- Master/Remote Selection
- Flash Exposure Bracketing
- Output Mode Selection (TTL, Manual, Stroboscopic)
- Modeling Flash
- AF Auto-Assist Beam
- Auto On/Off

High-Speed (FP) Sync

Your camera's shutter speed and the timing of the output of your flash must be synchronized. This is usually handled automatically when the flash is attached to the camera. Depending on the camera model and the shooting mode, the standard flash sync speed (shutter speed when using flash) might be no more than 1/200 or 1/250 of a second, which is fine where lighting conditions are generally low enough to require the use of flash.

A problem arises, however, when using flash in brighter conditions, as in outdoor portraits in daylight, where fill lighting is desired. Even with lower ISO settings and reasonably smaller apertures, daylight shots tend to require faster shutter speeds, exceeding the standard flash sync speed. To overcome this, some flash units are capable of accommodating shutter speeds up to the fastest available on your camera. High-Speed Sync (see Figure 2.8) makes this possible.

There is a drawback to using High-Speed Sync that results from the way the flash must work to make it possible. To understand this, you need to consider that the camera's normal flash sync speed coincides with the fastest shutter speed available where the entire frame is exposed at once. Since the shutter at this speed is fully open during exposure, the single burst of light from normal flash will expose the entire frame at once. However, faster shutter speeds are achieved through the use of a fast-moving slit created by the shutter curtain that exposes the image in sections as it moves from one end of the frame to the other. While one part of the image is being exposed, the other parts are blocked from the scene. This means, when using normal flash with a single burst of light lasting only milliseconds, that burst will only illuminate the part of the

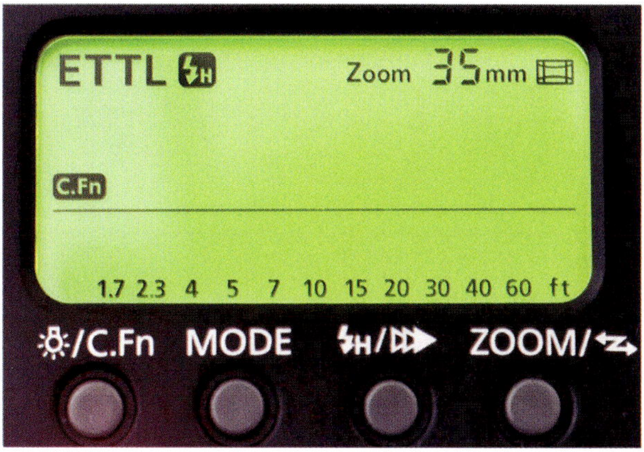

Figure 2.8
Flash LCD displaying High-Speed Sync.

image that is being exposed by the moving slit of the shutter; the part being blocked during the flash burst will not benefit from the flash at all.

The solution devised by flash technology engineers for this is to keep the flash illumination going for the duration of the exposure (which is relatively very long compared to a normal flash burst). High-Speed Sync accomplishes this by having the flash pulse several bursts of light for the duration of the exposure so that all parts of the image get some amount of flash. The downside is that the flash cannot pump out the full amount of light during each pulse, so overall flash output is diminished. Fortunately, it is still a workable solution for nearby subjects where only fill lighting is desired.

Front-/Rear-Curtain Sync

As stated earlier, the duration of the flash output is very short compared to the length of time the shutter is open during exposure. The burst of flash can be set to occur during the first part of the exposure (immediately after the shutter opens), or during the last part (immediately before the shutter closes). Normally, the flash is set to fire immediately following the opening of the leading, or front curtain of the shutter. If it's set to fire near the end of the exposure it is said to be synchronized with the shutter's trailing, or rear curtain.

What's important to know is that front- and rear-curtain sync can give you different effects having to do with the way the flash and the ambient light appear in your images. During longer exposures, when ambient, and other light, which is not coming from your flash, is strong enough to be recorded during exposure, it will "smudge" or "trail" as there is movement in the frame (either due to camera movement, movement in the scene, or both).

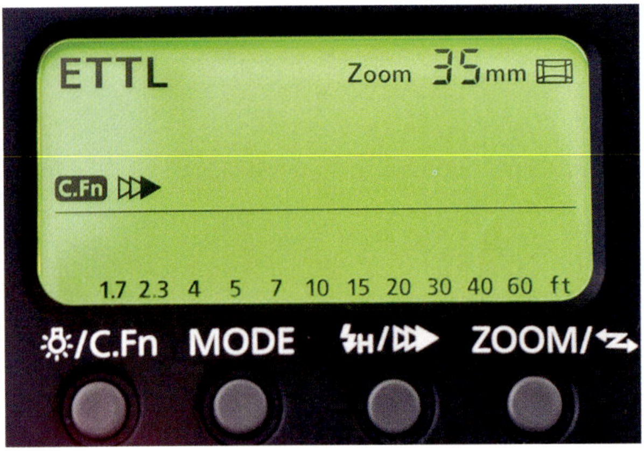

Figure 2.9
Flash LCD displaying rear-curtain sync.

Typically, the effect of ambient light is weaker than the flash illumination, but it also lasts longer. Because the flash illumination is so fast, it will appear to have frozen part of the image while other parts illuminated by ambient light will show signs of motion in the scene. The curtain sync, therefore determines when that "frozen" moment happens in the exposure.

For example, flash occurring during front-curtain sync will freeze the subject before most of the motion is recorded in the ambient light. If the subject is riding a bicycle at dusk, from left to right in the frame, he will appear most prominently on the left side, with a dimmer trail of himself recorded through to the right. That would look rather odd. On the other hand, using rear-curtain sync, ambient light records the bicyclist as he rides across the frame from left to right, with the flash exposing him at the end so he appears more prominently on the right, his "ghosted" image trailing behind him, which gives the effect of natural motion. A simple way to remember how this works is to associate *rear*-curtain sync with light trailing *behind* your subject.

Flash Exposure Compensation (FEC)

In TTL mode the light output of the flash is controlled automatically. This usually results in accurate flash exposures, but it doesn't always give you the desired outcome. With Flash Exposure Compensation (FEC), you can easily override the metering system and dial in more or less flash power as needed. FEC is often adjustable via a control dial on the flash unit itself, in the camera, or both.

Zoom

Some flash units are capable of narrowing the angle of the beam of light they emit. This has the benefit of focusing the light on a smaller area of the scene while increasing the light's intensity in that area. Where flash zoom is available, it can be adjusted automatically, and also manually with some units, to provide the correct angle of coverage for the lens being used, or in some cases, for a lighting effect.

Master/Remote Selection

Flash units capable of sending and receiving control signals to other flash units can act either as remote/slave units or as controller/master units. Via controls on each unit (see Figure 2.10), one flash (usually located on the camera) is designated "master" while the others are set to the remote/slave setting. The master unit gives you wireless TTL control over multiple remote flash units set at different positions and distances from the camera. Fine lighting control can be achieved by using features such as lighting ratios and groups. Some cameras are also capable of sending remote control signals to other flash units, via a "commander" mode, through their built-in pop-up flash or with special flash control attachments (e.g., Canon's Speedlite Transmitters). Most of these wireless systems use light or infrared pulses to communicate their control signals but Canon has introduced a flash unit that can transmit and receive radio TTL control signals. This eliminates line-of-sight limitations associated with light pulse signaling.

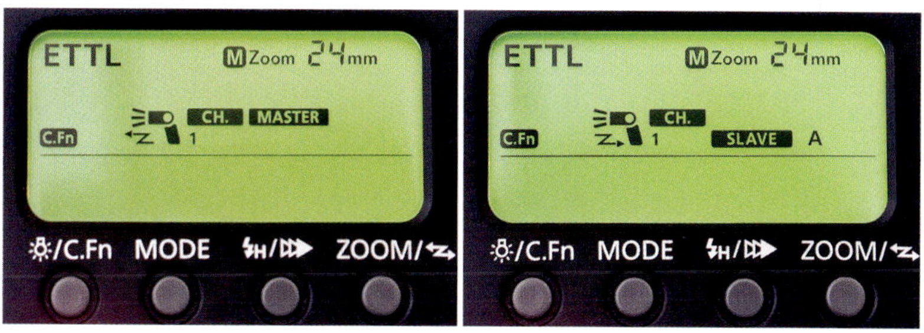

Figure 2.10 Flash LCD displaying Master and Slave/Remote settings.

Flash Exposure Bracketing (FEB)

Similar to the concept of exposure bracketing, FEB can be set to automatically adjust flash output over a series of shots, without affecting other exposure settings. Using your current flash output setting as a starting point, you can set FEB to give you two or three flash output levels for three different shots (e.g., –1 stop, normal, and +1 stop). Depending on the camera, the FEB setting might remain in force until zeroed out. This could become confusing, as the following exposures would be affected by seemingly inconsistent flash output levels.

FEB might be useful when you'd like to take some flash photos with more than one flash power level to choose from for a given shot. You'll have to take care not to run down your flash with too much FEB, and watch that you're not shooting before the flash is fully recycled. Rather than using FEB, you'll probably find that it's more useful to simply take a shot, make a quick visual evaluation off the LCD preview monitor and adjust the flash output as needed.

Flash Exposure/Value Lock (FEL/FV-Lock)

Using TTL, the output of your flash for each new photo taken is usually computed based on how the scene is metered. As you depress the shutter button to take a photo, a pre-flash fires which allows the camera to take a reading which determines the flash output necessary for the actual exposure. Next, the shutter opens and the previously calculated output is used to expose the subject. This works well for subjects located near the center portion of the scene. But there are times when you want to maintain a good flash exposure on a subject that is placed off-center in the composition. Flash Exposure Lock (FEL/FV-Lock) allows you to do this.

It is possible to have the camera memorize its setting for the TTL-controlled output of your flash for a scene, so you can then recompose and shoot one or more images based on the stored value. Here's how to use this feature:

1. Before taking the picture, place your subject in the middle of the frame in your viewfinder and press your camera's Flash Exposure Lock button. (This may go under different names based on your system's nomenclature. For example, Nikon uses the term, Flash Value (FV) Lock.)
2. A pre-flash fires, TTL calculates the correct exposure for the subject, and that information is stored in memory.
3. Without changing the actual distance from the flash to your subject, you are free to recompose so that they may appear anywhere in your shot. Press the shutter button to take the photo as usual.

Modeling Flash

With natural or constant light sources, it's easy to see the effect of light and shadow on your subject prior to taking a picture. But with flash, the burst of light illuminating your subject is so brief that it's difficult, if not impossible, to see its effects in real time. Modeling flash partially solves that problem by firing several flash bursts in rapid succession in order to give the effect of temporary constant light, allowing you to make out where the light and shadows will fall on your subject during the actual exposure. This is not actually used during exposure; it's a live previewing feature.

Modeling flash is probably not very useful for on-camera flash, and it must be used with caution as it can cause the flash to overheat and become damaged with too many consecutive bursts. In most situations, it's probably a better idea to take individual test shots using normal flash and simply refer to the camera's LCD preview monitor to view the results, making adjustments to the flash's position as necessary.

AF-Assist Beam

In low light, your flash can automatically output a small beam of light to help your camera automatically focus on the subject. This feature can be disabled if necessary.

Auto On/Off

As with many battery-powered devices, your flash may have a power conservation feature. If enabled, this puts your flash on standby or otherwise turns it off if it's been sitting idle for a few minutes. Depressing the shutter button or pressing a button on the flash will return it to a ready state.

Camera Modes and TTL

The automatic exposure modes on your digital camera can shield you from the complexities of exposure so that you can take on as little, or as much, control over the camera's options and settings as you like. Generally, the more automatic the mode is, the easier it makes the camera to use. However, it can be useful to trade some automation for more creative control, which is the case with camera modes like Aperture Priority and Shutter Priority, where you have deliberate control over one aspect of exposure, while the camera automatically adjusts other settings to compensate. For total creative control, your camera can also be operated in Manual mode.

Likewise, your flash has modes that allow for both automatic and manual output control. Coupled with your camera's shooting modes, you have plenty of options for controlling overall exposure, flash exposure, and background exposure. Your knowledgeable use of the available camera and flash modes will make them creative, flexible, and extensible tools.

If you want good flash exposures without having to manually meter or calculate flash output, then TTL is your best choice. This flash mode works well with all camera exposure modes from fully automatic to manual. The following is a list of the most commonly available camera shooting modes.

- Full Auto (green mode)
- Program mode (P)
- Aperture Priority mode (Av)
- Shutter Priority mode (Tv)
- Manual mode (M)
- Custom and other Program/Scene modes

Follow these steps to take advantage of TTL in the following camera modes:

1. Make sure the flash is properly attached to the camera and that both flash and camera are powered on.
2. Set your flash to TTL mode. (This might appear as "TTL," "ETTL," or similar depending on your flash manufacturer and model.)
3. Set your camera to one of modes listed below.
4. If given the option, make your selections for WB, ISO, and other settings.

Full Auto (Green) Mode

In Full Auto mode, your camera makes all the decisions concerning aperture, shutter speed, ISO, and many other settings. TTL handles the flash output, so your digital camera is as easy to use as any point-and-shoot. Full Auto mode coupled with TTL flash is great for general snapshot photography where control over your exposure settings isn't desired.

Program Mode (P)

When you want a little more control over your settings, Program mode opens up more options than Full Auto. When the flash is attached, the shutter speed and aperture are determined for you, but you can choose the ISO, use FEC, and control other settings. You'll have to keep in mind that some settings adjustments are going to be limited by other factors. Exposure Compensation

(EC), for instance, will be limited by the flash sync speed in effect, when using flash. Program mode is good for general photography when you'd like limited control over exposure settings.

Aperture Priority Mode (Av)

When you are primarily concerned with controlling depth-of-field (as is often the case in portraiture), then Aperture Priority mode is what you want. This mode allows you to specify the aperture setting while your camera automatically adjusts shutter speed to maintain proper ambient exposure. In effect, you are also controlling shutter speed as a consequence of adjusting the aperture. Wider apertures will call for faster shutter speeds, while smaller apertures demand slower shutter speeds, given a constant ISO.

With an attached flash in TTL mode, any speed at or below the camera's normal maximum flash sync speed is possible, and if High-Speed Sync is enabled, the full range of shutter speeds on your camera is available. For indoor flash photography, access to slower shutter speeds via EC gives you creative control over the look of the background or ambient light. For outdoor daylight flash photography, pleasing depth-of-field and fill-light are both possible and easy when TTL and High-Speed Sync are enabled. Aperture Priority mode is good for controlling depth-of-field in both indoor and outdoor portrait photography, while relying on your camera to manage shutter speed, and TTL to manage flash output.

Shutter Priority Mode (Tv)

When you are primarily concerned with controlling shutter speed, then Shutter Priority mode is what you want. Where Aperture Priority automatically adjusts the shutter speed as you control the aperture, Shutter Priority mode automatically adjusts the aperture setting as you alter the shutter speed.

With an attached flash using TTL, any speed at or below the flash sync is possible, and if High-Speed Sync is enabled, the full range of shutter speeds on your camera is available. Using Shutter Priority indoors may cause your camera to give you underexposure warnings when the combination of your selected shutter speed and the lens's widest aperture aren't enough to give a proper exposure to the ambient light. This will happen even though good flash exposures are still possible and the flash is likely to add to the final light mix in the background.

Shutter Priority mode is good for sports or other action photography where maintaining a fast shutter speed is more important than specifying depth-of-field.

Manual Mode (M)

Interestingly, TTL also works when your camera is in Manual mode. In fact, this is one of the most powerful combinations of camera/flash modes. In this case, you maintain full control over your digital camera's settings, like aperture, shutter speed and ISO, but TTL still controls flash output for you. TTL tries to give you the best flash exposure for your subject, given your camera settings.

Because there are limitations to the flash's minimum and maximum output, the results of TTL's efforts are dependent on your actual camera settings. For example, if you have your aperture set to f/1.8 and your ISO to 6400, chances are good that TTL will not be able to prevent the flash from overexposing your subject. In this scenario, TTL would likely use the flash's lowest possible output setting, which might still result in overexposure using those camera settings.

Note

In all modes, including Manual mode, if an attached external flash unit is powered on the camera will not allow you to use a shutter speed that exceeds the flash sync speed unless you are using High-Speed Sync.

Manual mode is good for indoor photography where easy control over the ambient light is possible by adjusting the shutter speed dial (see Chapter 4).

Other Program/Easy Modes

If your camera has specific use program modes, such as Portrait, Sports, or special Guide/Scene modes, etc., these can be handy to use, too. You'll have to experiment with each one to see which settings are imposed by the camera in those modes, and which you are allowed to adjust to your liking. In any event, TTL should manage flash output quite nicely for you. If you feel a program mode is limiting, you can opt for Aperture Priority, Shutter Priority, or Manual.

Camera Modes and Manual Flash

Unlike TTL, your flash's Manual mode allows you to set the power output of your flash independent of any metering. If you want the flash to fire at 1/8 power or full power, that's up to you; with Manual flash, there is no automatic control to govern the output. So, no matter what mode your camera is set to, the flash will fire at the power output you set manually (unless, of course, your camera overrides Manual flash mode, which is likely the case when your digital camera is set to Full Auto mode). Using Manual flash generally means that changes to ISO, aperture, and distance from your subject will have an effect on your flash exposures. This is because changes to any of these factors would normally require the flash output to be adjusted, and flash output otherwise stays constant when the flash is in Manual mode. As a rule, TTL is actually better suited to most camera program modes. Using an automatic camera mode with manual flash is not only counter-intuitive, but generally more trouble than it's worth (you generally can't even set your flash to Manual with the camera in Full Auto mode). Manual flash is therefore most useful when used with your digital camera's Manual exposure mode.

Manual Mode (M) and Manual Flash

Your camera's Manual mode is the most appropriate exposure mode when using Manual flash. In this case, you maintain full control over your camera's settings, like aperture, shutter speed, and ISO, as well as full control over flash output. Since there is no automatic exposure or flash output control, you are responsible for keeping everything in balance to achieve the exposure you want.

While your camera is likely equipped with an exposure level indicator to help you adjust settings for ambient exposure, you're on your own for determining flash output. This is often accomplished with a hand-held flash exposure meter (see Chapter 3), or simply by taking test shots and making flash power setting adjustments until the proper settings are determined.

Chapter 3

Flash Gear and Accessories

Although you might think the easiest way to get proper exposures from your flash is to mount it directly on your camera in standard straight-ahead position, it is only one of several techniques to explore. But as with most things in photography, technique is often closely tied to, if not dependent on, our tools and gear. In order to apply traditional portrait lighting with flash, for instance, you'll first have to mount your flash on a stand and modify the light for effect.

Having a basic toolbox of flash-related gear and attachments will open up new possibilities for your flash photography. Before we explore those possibilities, two basic flash techniques should be discussed.

Two Basic Flash Techniques

Direct, on-camera flash and bounce flash are basic flash techniques that don't require the use of flash modifiers like diffusion attachments or bounce cards. Those accessories are extremely useful tools to have on hand, but you should first become acquainted with the techniques you can use to get great shots when only one on-camera, unmodified flash unit is available.

Direct Flash

Although many flash enthusiasts will tell you that direct, on-camera flash (see Figure 3.1) is a "no-no," that isn't necessarily true. It's actually a widely used look for everything from event photo booth shots to magazine covers and fashion ads. Yes, direct flash can be harsh and contrasty, but it can also evoke a sense of excitement and urgency. It's entirely possible to create a bold, powerful portrait and good group shots with direct, on-camera flash. It can be most effective when your subject is positioned a very short distance from the

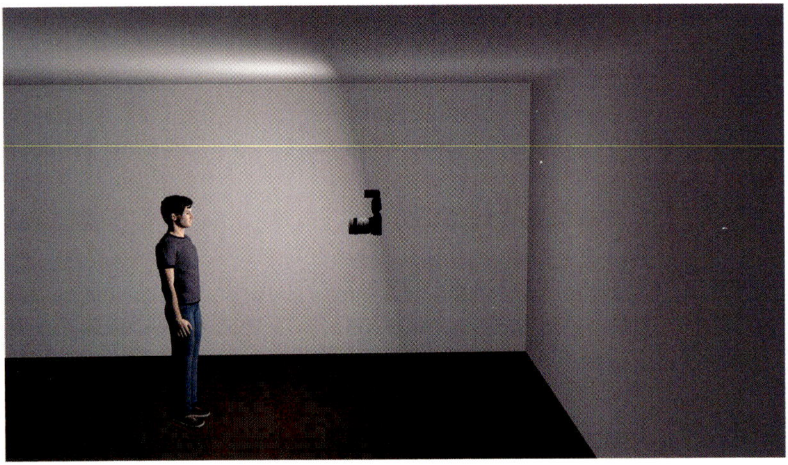

Figure 3.1 The normal flash position (left) will result in the subject receiving direct flash.

background, where a background surface is absent, or when used very subtly for outdoor fill light.

Be aware that using on-camera flash in the normal position while your camera is in the vertical shooting position can cause a noticeable side lighting effect which is not always desirable. Camera-mounted flash can also create flare effects in reflective surfaces behind your subject (directly opposite your flash).

Bounce Flash

Direct flash has its place in the list of basic flash techniques, but much of the time it can result in harsh, unflattering portraits. Fortunately, most mid- to high-end flash units are equipped with flash heads that are capable of tilting up to 90 degrees while simultaneously rotating up to 180 degrees to the right and/or left. Depending on the environment, this allows for a creative use of bounce flash which can greatly improve the look of your pictures.

By aiming the flash off the camera axis so that its light strikes a large light-colored surface (like a wall and/or ceiling), the relatively small and harsh light coming from the flash is transformed into a large and diffuse glow, illuminating the environment and your subjects more evenly. As you prepare to shoot a photo in a normal-sized room for instance, tilt your flash head so that it points up about 45 degrees, then rotate it 180 degrees as shown in Figure 3.2. This will cause the flash to illuminate a large area of the wall and ceiling behind you, which will then evenly illuminate the room.

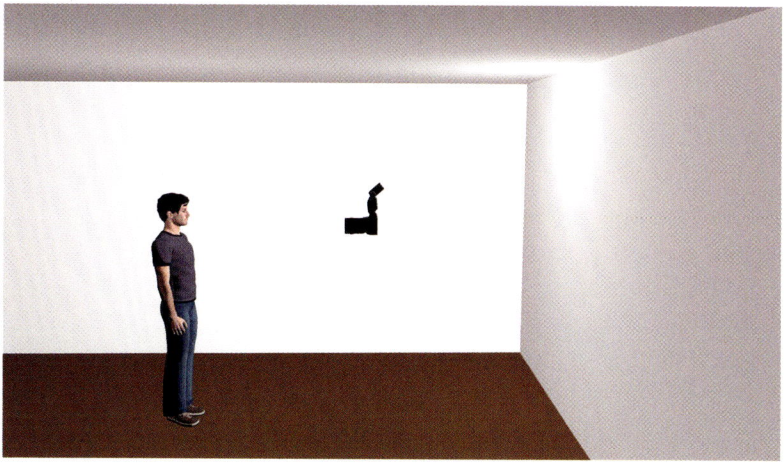

Figure 3.2 With a flash unit capable of having its head rotated 180 degrees and tilted up (right), you can achieve pleasing bounce flash illumination off the wall and ceiling surfaces behind you.

TTL is capable of metering and controlling flash output when the flash is not striking the subject directly, so you are free to bounce the flash illumination and still benefit from TTL's automatic flash control. Creative use of bounce flash will be covered in detail in Chapter 4.

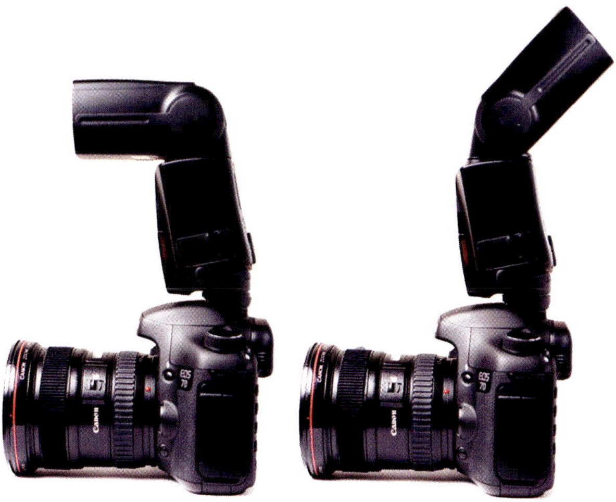

Figure 3.3 On-camera flash shown in normal forward-facing position (left) and in bounce position (right).

On-Camera Flash Accessories

Your flash is a powerful source of light, designed to provide good results for general use. However, when used in the normal, forward-facing position, it can create rather harsh and unflattering illumination, especially for portraiture. Tilting and rotating the flash head solves most of the problems associated with direct flash, but there are a few accessories available that can help you make the most of your on- and off-camera flash photography:

- Bounce Cards
- Flags
- Snoots
- Diffusion Attachments
- Brackets
- Color Gels
- Specialty Modifiers
- Off-Camera Gear

Bounce Cards

A bounce card can be a white piece of cardboard, crafting foam, or other material that can be placed on the end of a flash unit to help redirect some of the flash's output toward the subject. As a flash modifier, the bounce card is effective in two ways: First, it reflects an area of light that is larger than just the flash lens alone, onto the subject. As bounce flash demonstrates, a larger light source relative to the subject provides more pleasing light. Second, the main beam of the flash is directed toward the ceiling for additional bounce within the room. This sets up an efficient and very effective use of on-camera bounce flash.

You can make your own bounce card by cutting a piece of flexible craft foam in the shape shown in Figure 3.4. Cut an 8" square from the top corners at an angle so that the base ends up approximately 5" in length. To use the bounce card:

1. In order to use the bounce card correctly when the camera is in the vertical shooting position, it must fit on the flash head as shown in Figure 3.4. The bounce card is actually secured to the side of the flash head, not the back as you might expect.
2. For horizontal shooting, make sure the flash head is pointed straight up with the surface of the bounce card facing your subject. This allows the light from the flash to reflect off the bounce card directly onto your subject, as well as off the ceiling for more scattered, soft illumination.
3. For vertical shots, flip the flash head as you turn the camera to the vertical position so that the bounce card maintains its standard vertical position. Again, the subject will benefit from a wider flash reflection off the bounce card, as well as the ceiling bounce.

> **Note**
>
> The built-in white card that comes with some flash units is not meant to serve as a bounce card modifier as we've described. Built-in reflectors of this type are primarily useful for creating catchlights in the eyes when the flash head is in a 45 degree or higher tilt position.

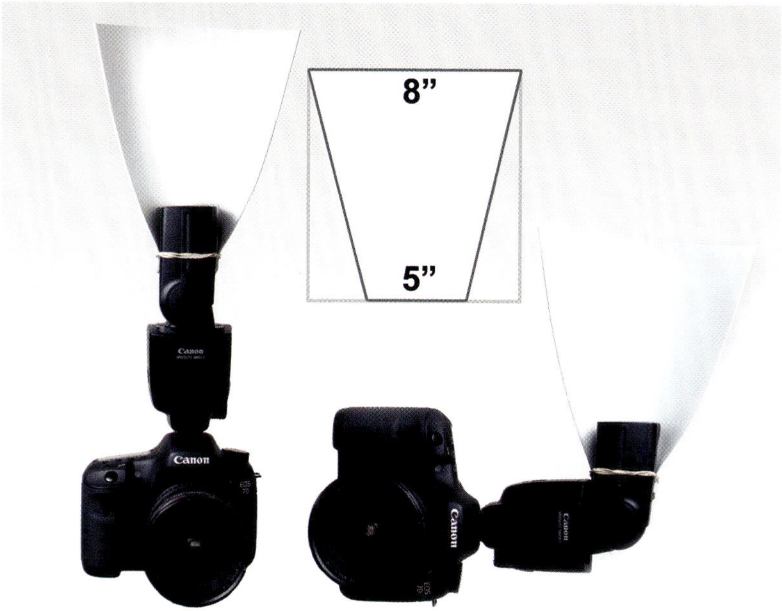

Figure 3.4 A simple bounce card shown in horizontal and vertical shooting modes. This bounce card is made from an 8" × 8" piece of crafting foam cut into the shape shown in the inset and attached with a standard rubber band. Commercial variations of this are also available.

Flags

A flag is used to help block light from spilling or flaring out in directions you don't want it to. We can take this concept and apply it to our flash unit. Since light from a flash shoots out at a wider angle than you'd expect, it can be helpful to place a small flag on one side of the flash head as shown in Figure 3.5 to keep the light that's coming directly off the flash from hitting the subject when using, for instance, a flash bounce technique.

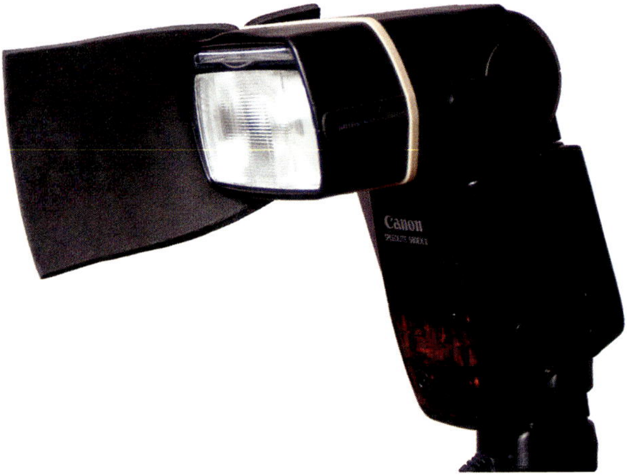

Figure 3.5
A small flag made of black crafting foam secured to the flash head with a rubber band.

Snoots

For even more directional control of the flash output, a snoot (see Figure 3.6) can be fashioned out of any flexible opaque material and placed on the flash head to narrow the beam of light emitted.

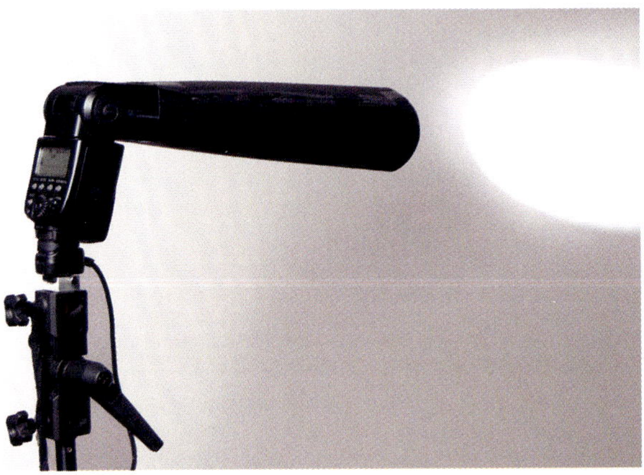

Figure 3.6
Snoot made of black construction paper.

Diffusion Attachments

A diffusion attachment helps spread the light from your flash around the room so that it bounces off of more surfaces than with the flash unit alone. This creates softer, more pleasing illumination for your images. Diffusion attachments are usually made of plastic and fit right on the end of your flash head.

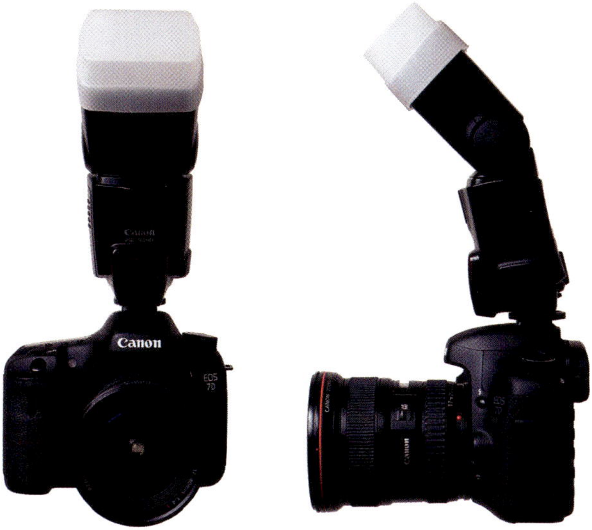

Figure 3.7
A diffusion attachment placed on the flash head in the recommended position.

Once attached, the flash head is generally titled 45 degrees or more to maximize the potential bounce, as shown in Figure 3.7.

One type of attachment that is often referred to as a flash diffuser is the so-called mini-softbox. This type of flash modifier does create a limited amount of diffusion as it, in effect, creates a larger light surface than the lens of the flash unit itself. It is more directional than a diffusion attachment like the plastic cover type shown here, however, and not designed to help you bounce light around the room. The most noticeable results from a mini-softbox are achieved when used at close range.

Brackets

Another way to raise the flash output from the standard on-camera hot shoe position is to use a flash bracket attachment (see Figure 3.8). Some brackets allow you to orient the flash a number of ways around the camera body. Not for everyone, flash brackets still keep the flash relatively close to the lens axis and may be cumbersome to use. One of the main advantages of using a bracket is that it allows you to keep the flash unit above the camera, rather than to the side, for vertical shooting. Generally, you'd follow these steps to set up your flash bracket:

1. Mount the camera to the bracket. Secure the bottom of the camera to the bracket by placing the end of the mounting screw into the camera's tripod mount connector and turning the knob to fasten.

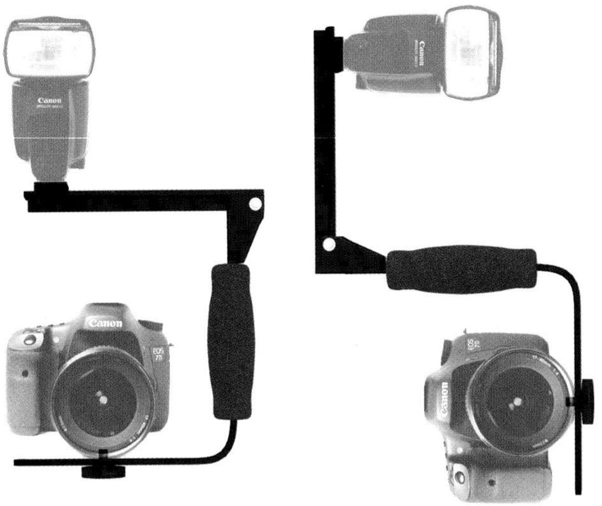

Figure 3.8
Flash brackets like this allow you to mount the flash slightly higher than the on-camera position. A pivoting arm keeps the flash above the lens in both horizontal and vertical shooting positions.

2. Attach a sync cord or triggering device to your flash, and then mount the flash to the flash shoe on the bracket.
3. Attach the other end of the sync chord, or triggering device, to the camera.

Color Gels

If you're familiar with the White Balance (WB) setting on your camera, you know that natural and artificial light can vary in color temperature, creating color casts in your images. The WB setting allows you to compensate for a potential color cast by selecting the appropriate "light type" from the available choices. Options generally include: Auto, Sunlight, Shade, Cloudy, Tungsten, Florescent, Flash, and Custom. Without the proper WB adjustments, pictures taken under household tungsten light may appear orange, or too blue if taken in the shade, or greenish if under traditional florescent tubes.

But the WB setting can only match one color temperature at a time. If you're using flash indoors together with ambient tungsten lighting, which WB setting do you use, Flash or Tungsten? If you use the Flash setting, the tungsten lighting might appear too warm and orange in the shot while parts with more flash illumination appear white. If you use the Tungsten setting, the ambient light will appear closer to white, but the flash illumination will look too blue.

One solution is to match the color of the flash to the surrounding ambient light and use the correct WB setting for that color, in this case tungsten. You can change the color your flash emits by placing a Color Temperature Orange (CTO) gel over the lens of the flash. This will match the light emitted from it to tungsten. Likewise, attaching a greenish filter (often called Window Green) to your flash helps match it up to traditional florescent lighting. Under this scenario, you'd simply change your WB setting to florescent. There is no need to alter the color of your flash under daylight, or near daylight illumination because the flash is already in that color temperature range.

Gels (see Figure 3.9) can be purchased and cut to size, if necessary, to fit over the lens of your flash secured by tape, rubber bands, or Velcro. Color-correcting light modifiers which serve the same purpose are also available.

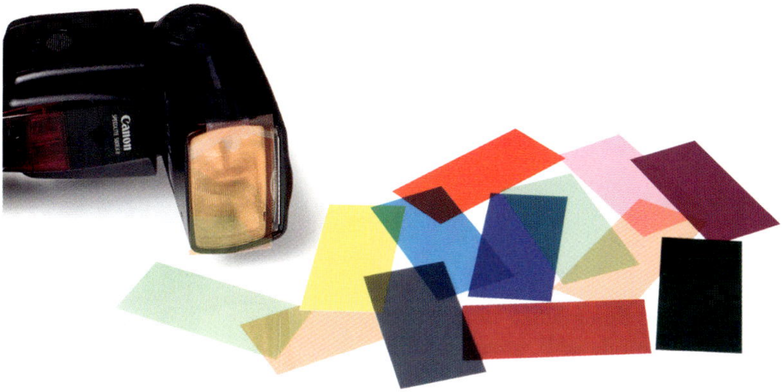

Figure 3.9 These correction and effect gels are pre-cut to 1.5" × 3.25". The flash shown here has a Color Temperature Orange (CTO) gel secured over its lens with tape. Directly in front of this is a green gel for balancing the flash to florescent ambient light. Other gels are available for flash color effects.

Specialty Modifiers

There are an ever growing number of flash modifiers that range from the useful to specialty/novelty, to ridiculous. Some popular attachments turn flash units into mini studio lights. These include ring lights, grids and snoots, and true off-camera softboxes. There are also attachments available which claim to offer a great variety of modification settings but are clumsy in design and functionality. Some modifiers, it must be said, are just too silly looking to use and offer little advantage over traditional solutions to make them worthwhile. Our best advice is to stick to modifiers of simple design and functionality.

Off-Camera and Multiple Flash

Modifiers and bounce techniques are great, but even more control is possible with the ability to position a flash unit anywhere around your subject, independent of your camera position. If you have multiple flash units compatible with the same TTL system, you can set them up in easy to manage, limitless configurations, to illuminate your subject and scene in creative ways. See your documentation for the specifics of how to set up multiple flashes with your system. Many systems allow you to do one or more of the following:

- **Built-in flash + one or more remote external flash units.** Use your camera's built-in flash as both an on-camera flash and "commander" with one or more remote flash units. Settings on the camera allow you to adjust the lighting ratios between the flashes to your liking, as TTL maintains overall flash exposure control (see Figure 3.10).
- **Flash controller unit + one or more remote external flash units.** Flash controller units like Canon's Speedlite Transmitter (ST-E2) shown here, are mounted on the camera's hot shoe and provide a set of controls for one or more flashes and flash groups (see Figure 3.11). The ST-E2 does not provide any flash output of its own.
- **Flash unit on-camera + one or more remote external flash units.** The flash unit mounted on your camera serves as the master unit and controls one or more off-camera flashes and flash groups, designated as remote/slave units (see Figure 3.12). The master flash can have its flash output set to "off" so that it controls the remote units without contributing any flash output of its own to the exposure. This is useful for images where you don't want noticeable flash illumination coming in from the camera position.

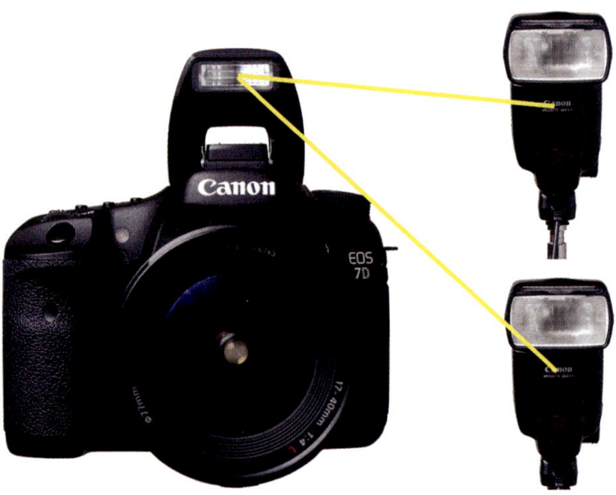

Figure 3.10
Built-in flash controlling one or more flash units.

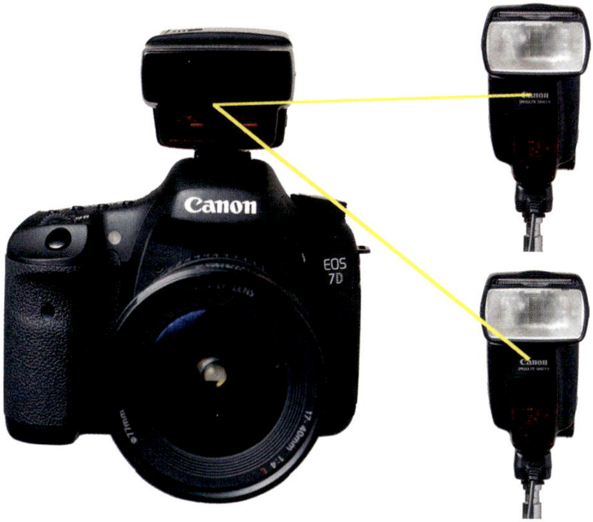

Figure 3.11
Flash controller unit controlling one or more flash units.

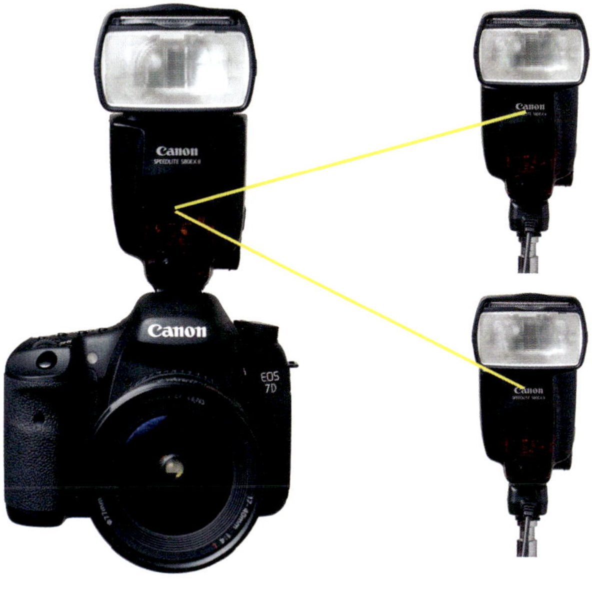

Figure 3.12
Flash unit controlling one or more other flash units.

Next, we'll discuss what you'll need to set up your flash unit(s) off-camera and how to modify your flash units with photography lighting umbrellas, effectively turning your flash into studio quality lighting.

TTL Enabled Off-Camera Flash Gear

Achieving more sophisticated flash portraiture and other types of photography is easily accomplished with off-camera flash in TTL mode. TTL maintains proper flash exposure for one or more flash units and even gives you the creative freedom to balance the output of individual flash units, or groups, to your liking. The following are recommended for off-camera TTL flash:

- TTL Master/Controller Unit
- Light Stand or Other Flash Support
- Flash Mount Adapter
- Umbrella Modifier
- TTL Sync Cord

TTL Master/Controller Unit

As described in the previous section, you can control compatible, off-camera flash units with either your camera's built-in flash (via a commander mode or similar), a dedicated flash control transmitter (see Figure 3.13), or a flash unit designated as the master of the off-camera remote units.

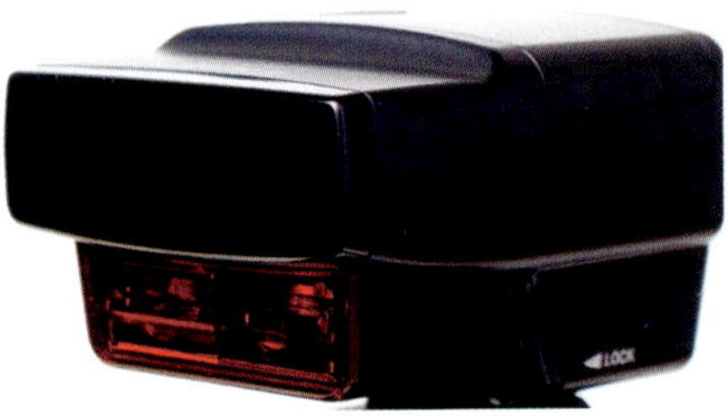
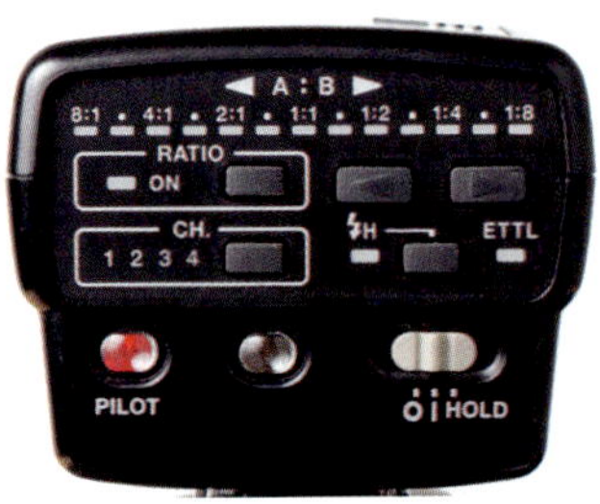

Figure 3.13 A wireless flash controller like the Canon ST-E2 shown here, attaches to the hot shoe of a Canon dSLR. It can control a single flash or multiple units for TTL operation. Some cameras provide similar functionality via menu controls and built-in flash.

Light Stand or Other Support

You need some support or stand to secure your off-camera flash. For a short series of photos, you might be able to have an assistant hold a flash unit for you at the desired height and angle. This can be done by holding the flash in-hand, or as it's secured to a monopod or some other support. However, you'll get more consistent lighting, and be able to use light modifiers and other gear by using proper light stands. Any standard or lightweight collapsible stand will do

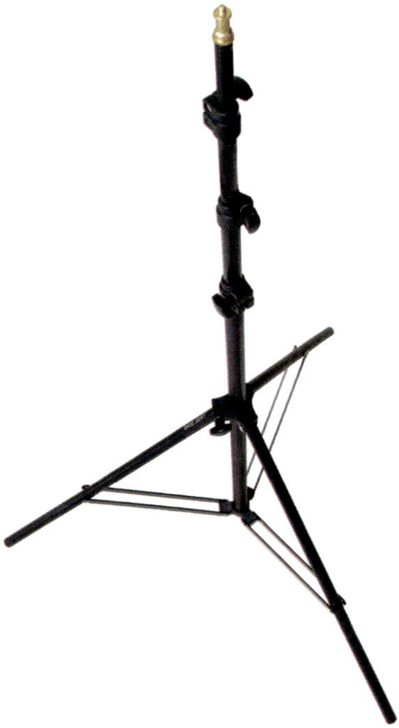

Figure 3.14
Lightweight collapsible light stand.

(see Figure 3.14), but the sturdier the better, and it should be able to extend to a height of at least seven feet. A stud is usually set at the top of the stand which allows you to mount flash attachments and adapters.

Flash Mount Adapter, Umbrella Adapter

In order to mount your flash unit on a light stand, you'll need some type of mounting adapter. A flash umbrella adapter as shown in Figure 3.15, attaches to the light stand on one end and allows the flash to be mounted on the other. This adapter secures the flash to the stand and provides swivel/tilting functionality and a place to mount an external light modifier, such as an umbrella. To mount it to the light stand:

1. Fit the bottom end of the adapter onto the light stand stud as shown in Figure 3.16. Tighten the adapter to the stud using the tightening knob.
2. If your adapter does not have a flash mounting shoe already in place, you will have to attach one. Fit the flash mounting shoe onto the adapter (in Figure 3.15, the shoe is attached to a stud which fits into the adapter) and tighten.

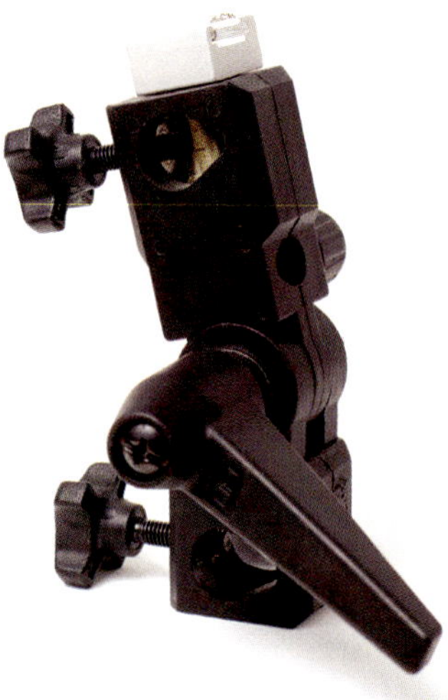

Figure 3.15 A flash umbrella-mounting adapter is a versatile piece of gear. This adapter fits on a light stand and allows you to mount an off-camera/remote flash unit and, optionally, a photographic lighting umbrella.

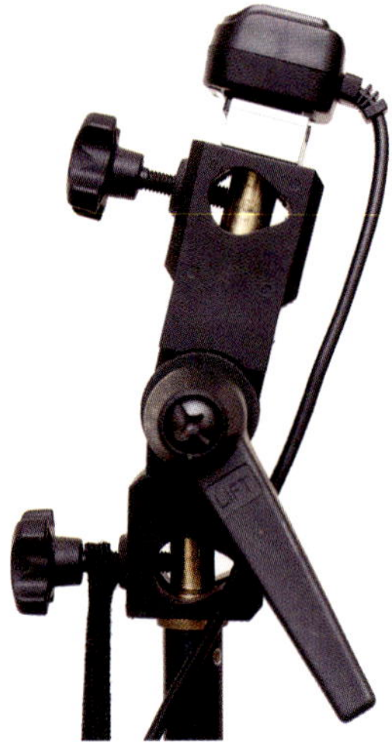

Figure 3.16 Umbrella adapter mounted on a light stand. The dark-colored adapter on top allows the flash to connect to a radio trigger (here, located below the swivel lever, just out of frame).

3. The hole for the umbrella is angled so that the swivel adjustment lever or knob is usually located on the right side for adjustments. This means that when you insert the umbrella shaft into the adapter, the lever is on the right side as you face the inside of the open umbrella.
4. The flash will be attached to the top of the umbrella adapter. If the flash is mounted on a triggering adapter, then the triggering adapter likely has a flash-type foot that can be mounted on the umbrella adapter shoe. The flash should be facing the umbrella.

Umbrella Modifier

When using an umbrella adapter as described above, a standard photographic lighting umbrella can be attached to the light stand (see Figure 3.17). The flash is pointed toward the inside of the umbrella, which serves to bounce a wider area of light back out, onto the subject. Another popular way to use an umbrella is as a diffuser for a softbox lighting effect. Here, a translucent white umbrella is pointed opposite the bounce orientation. The top of the umbrella is aimed toward the subject with the flash still pointing into it. When the flash fires, the light from the flash is emitted through the translucent material more evenly and over a larger surface area than the flash could have managed alone.

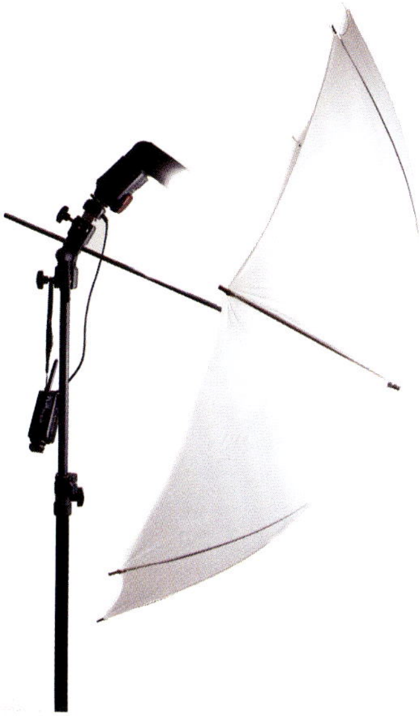

Figure 3.17
A white translucent umbrella is used to allow the flash to shine through it in the direction of the subject.

Note that when using modifiers or anything that might disrupt TTL light pulse communication signals between a master unit and remotes, you might have to reposition or reconfigure the flash units and/or head orientation. Fortunately, in most indoor environments and shooting situations, these types of TTL signals are able to bounce around enough to reach their targets with no problem. Outdoor use of TTL seems to pose a bit of a problem because of the lack of signal bounce and the brighter ambient light. TTL signals transmitted by radio (as with a new system by Canon, and some solutions offered by other manufacturers) eliminate this problem.

Softbox Modifier

A small softbox like the 2' × 2' model shown in Figure 3.18 is a great outdoor alternative to an umbrella. The wind can wreak havoc on an umbrella and bring down an entire light stand with it. A softbox can be mounted on a light stand, or a monopod which allows an assistant to hold and maneuver it easily.

Several types are available including ones that mount one or more flash units inside the softbox housing and some that are designed so that the flash sits outside for easy access. The benefits to having the flash mounted outside the softbox include wireless TTL use when light pulse communication is necessary, and being able to make manual mode adjustments without having to open up the softbox to reach the flash.

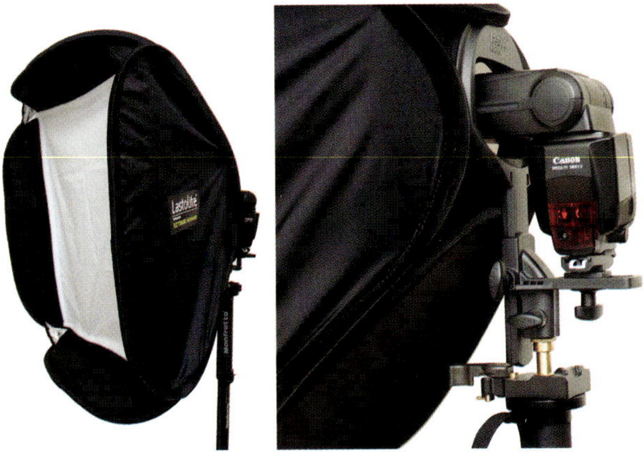

Figure 3.18
Softbox designed for use with shoe-mount flashes. Great for outdoor shooting as these tend to be much easier to control in the wind.

TTL Sync Cord

If wireless sync is not necessary, but moving the flash off the camera axis is desired, you can opt to use a dedicated TTL cord (see Figure 3.19) compatible with your system. These cords are configured with contacts that match the camera manufacturer's for TTL communication. One end of the cord fits on the dSLR's hot shoe, while the other is connected to the flash foot. These cords are useful in combination with flash brackets and anytime you'd like to have the flash a short distance from the camera, but still maintain a standard TTL connection.

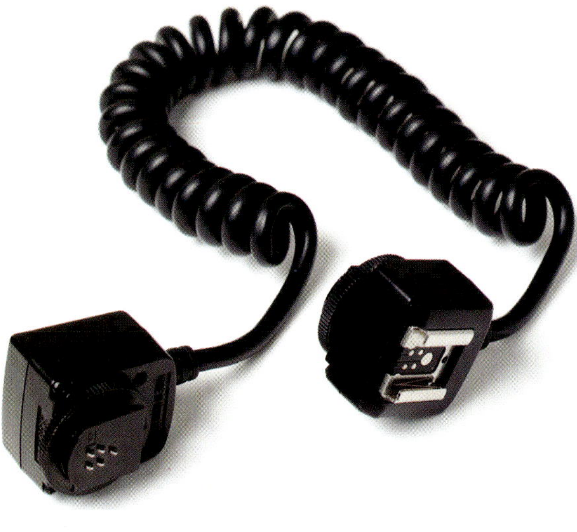

Figure 3.19
TTL flash sync cord.

Manual Off-Camera Flash Gear

When you want direct control over flash output, you can switch both your camera and flash unit(s) to manual mode. In manual mode, you'll have to judge the proper camera and flash output settings and determine your adjustments by viewing test shots on the LCD monitor, or you can use a hand-held light/flash meter to take measurements and determine settings before making exposures. Here are a few things that can be combined with some of the gear in the previous section to help make off-camera manual flash more successful for you:

- Flash Exposure Meter
- Built-in Wireless Trigger
- Radio Trigger
- Sync Cables

Flash Exposure Meter

Hand-held flash meters (light meters) are not relied on as much as they used to be in the days of film cameras. Digital photography and the LCD preview monitor have made it easy to quickly evaluate the effects of lighting, and changes in lighting, in a scene without the use of an external light meter. However, a light meter can still be a valuable tool for quickly determining ambient exposure and/or manual flash exposure and power settings. It can help maintain lighting consistency and aid in determining and reproducing specific lighting ratios. Even where off-camera metering isn't technically necessary, some photographers prefer to use a flash meter according to their working style.

Light meters, like the one shown in Figure 3.20, usually allow measurements to be taken in two general modes:

- **Reflected (or Reflective).** This mode of metering is essentially the same as what the camera's internal exposure meter does when measuring ambient (not flash) lighting in the scene. The light meter measures the light being reflected off the scene or subject from the perspective of the camera. The area being measured can be large, which will give you an average reading. By placing the meter closer to smaller areas of the scene, the meter will measure those smaller areas individually giving you similar functionality to a camera's spot metering. When shooting with a camera with a built-in exposure meter this type of external metering is redundant.

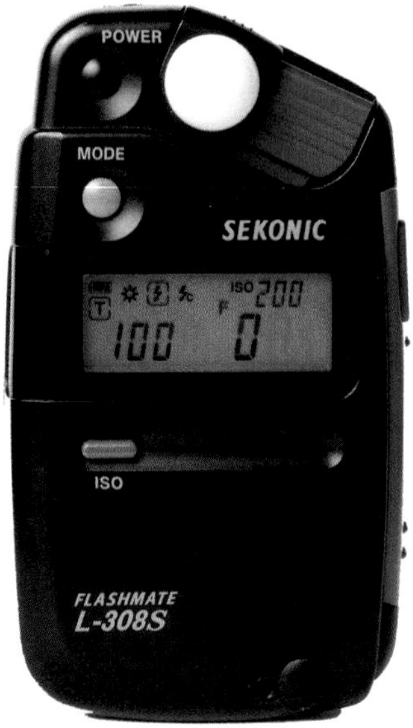

Figure 3.20
A flash/light meter is helpful for determining the correct flash output and camera exposure settings when using manual camera and flash modes.

- **Incident.** This mode of metering is useful for taking accurate flash readings from the position of the subject. The light meter (as flash meter) measures the light from the flash that is striking the subject, not the light that is being reflected off the subject. In other words, it measures the light coming from the light source directly. It allows you to measure the light coming from individual light sources, or the combination of more than one light source. When using a light meter in Incident mode, a white dome-like surface covers the meter's lens. This allows the meter to read light coming in from a wide angle.

Using a Flash Meter

Of course, you should consult the documentation for your model of flash exposure meter to learn how to use it for your needs. But there are some basics to get you started using it with Manual flash.

Incident light metering, used with flash photography, places the meter not at the location of the camera, but at the location of the subject. Start by making sure your light meter is set to Incident metering mode. Metering is achieved by placing the light dome cover over the meter's lens (if detachable), holding the meter very near the subject, and pointing it back toward the camera. Clicking the measuring button will tell the meter to wait for a flash of light, which it will measure when you fire the flash unit(s), either via test firing or with an actual test shot. What you're attempting to measure is the flash of light at the position the light meter is located. Depending on where you place your meter, you're trying to get an idea of how the light is affecting your subject and other areas of the image, including the background.

Assuming a portrait setup with one or more flash units and your camera all set to Manual, a basic flash reading is taken like this:

1. Have your flash units on, set to an initial power setting (e.g., 1/8 power), and positioned where you want them.
2. Your flash meter should be on, in Incident mode, with the lens dome over the electric eye/lens. Make sure the flash meter is set to measure based on the same ISO your camera is set to.
3. Have the subject, or an assistant, hold the meter just inches in front of the subject's face, with the dome facing the camera. There should be nothing obscuring the flash from the meter.
4. Press the flash meter's ready button, and then take a test shot which should fire the flash unit(s).
5. Note the reading on the flash meter. It should specify the correct aperture and shutter speed combination for a good exposure, based on the ISO provided.

For photographers who need to get their portrait lighting set up quickly, a flash meter can be indispensable. It should be noted that each individual flash unit can be measured independently by pointing the flash meter in the direction of each flash during separate test firings. This is handy if you want to measure individual output settings for the purpose of setting up specific lighting ratios, so use whatever method works best for you.

Of course, a flash meter isn't always necessary if you use simple flash setups. A few quick test shots and quick evaluation of the results on your LCD preview monitor should help you make accurate adjustments to your light output or exposure settings as needed.

Built-in Wireless Trigger

Although TTL signals aren't available when your flash units are in manual mode, the built-in flash, or the unit directly connected to your camera can still trigger the other units to flash in sync with the exposure. If your dSLR can do this with its built-in flash, you can access wireless control of compatible flash units via the camera's menu. An external flash with this capability will also have a switch and/or menu controls that set the flash up as the master unit.

Radio Triggers

A radio trigger system (see Figure 3.21), consisting of a transmitter and one or more receivers, is capable of transmitting a flash sync signal farther and more dependably than the camera's wireless light signals. The transmitter is the unit (connected to the camera) that sends out a signal to the receiver units (each one connected to a remote flash). When the camera shutter is clicked, the radio transmitter fires all remote flashes on the designated channel. Some radio triggers are capable of retransmitting and receiving TTL messages, but traditionally, they've been used as simple triggering devices for use with manual flash. Basic, non-TTL radio triggers are described in this section.

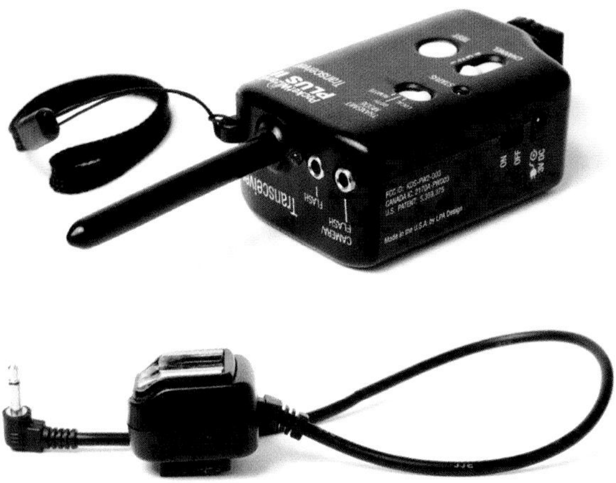

Figure 3.21
Radio trigger (top). A similar looking unit which serves as a transmitter is mounted to the camera's hot shoe. Flash-to-receiver adapter cord (bottom). The flash is mounted to the adapter cord and the adapter cord is then mounted to the umbrella adapter on the light stand.

Since basic radio triggers do not send or receive TTL information between the camera and flash units, you will be using your remote flashes in Manual mode. This will require you to use a shutter speed no faster than the dSLR's rated flash sync speed and you'll need to do test shots and/or flash metering to determine the proper flash output and camera settings.

Although non-TTL radio triggers come in many varieties with different features, their main use is straightforward:

1. Connect a receiver unit to a remote flash, making sure that both the flash and receiver are off. Some radio trigger receivers have a shoe you can mount the flash to, while others require a corded connection, which means some type of adapter might be needed to connect the flash to the radio trigger receiver. If your receiver has a channel selector, make sure it is set to the channel you want it to operate on. Repeat this with each remote flash that you want to trigger with the master transmitter.

2. With the camera and radio trigger transmitter both off, connect the radio trigger transmitter unit to the camera. Most units are designed to be mounted to the camera's hot shoe. If your transmitter has a channel selector, make sure it is set to the channel you want it to operate on.
3. Turn on all flash triggering devices (transmitter and receivers).
4. Turn on the camera and all flash units. (While it may not actually be necessary to power on the various components in this way, it will help prevent unnecessary flash firing.)
5. Select the desired Manual output settings on the flash units as well as the Manual exposure settings on your dSLR.
6. If your transmitter has a test button, you may want to press it to check that your flash units are all firing as expected. If you notice a misfire, check the connections, batteries, and settings at the misfiring units.

Flash Sync Cords

Non-TTL corded sync is available with PC cords. To use these, both camera and flash must have some way to connect the cord—either through a built-in connector or an adapter. One end of the PC cord is attached to the camera's PC terminal or adapter, and the other end is attached to a flash unit's PC connector or adapter. As with basic radio triggers, all that is transmitted is a simple signal that tells the flash when to fire. The camera is usually set to Manual mode, as is the flash (External Auto is also possible with some units). If multiple flash units are employed, the other flash units can be fired if they have optical slave triggers attached or built in.

Chapter 4

Indoor Flash Photography

Indoor flash photography offers the potential for great creative control over the look of your images. By using simple light modifiers and applying the principles of bounce lighting, you can spread the light around for more pleasing, softer illumination. But, indoor photography is often just as much about the flash as it is about the ambient light (e.g., room lamps, candles, accent lighting). These other light sources also illuminate the environment and can give your shots a better sense of atmosphere if captured correctly. Without taking ambient lighting into consideration, you might end up with images featuring dark backgrounds or cold flash lighting that look nothing like what you perceived with your own eyes. In this section, we'll cover some important indoor flash photography considerations, and show you several techniques to get you started.

Initial Settings for Indoor Flash Photography

We recommend that you adopt a regular starting point for your settings and controls. A standardized approach will give you the confidence of knowing exactly where you should start every time you use flash indoors. One way to remember our suggested method is by thinking of it as "fast and wide." The ISO and shutter speed are set to their fastest acceptable settings and your aperture is set to its widest acceptable f/stop, as determined by you ahead of time. Here are some tips for developing your personal indoor flash photography standardized approach:

- **Use your camera in Manual mode for creative control.** For quick-and-easy flash photography, you can follow the instructions in Chapter 1 and employ Full Auto or Program mode features. But for more creative control indoors, we recommend setting your camera to Manual mode. This will allow you to set the ISO, aperture, and shutter speed rather than letting the camera take control. This is especially important if you want to control the look of the ambient light in the environment—an important factor in indoor flash photography.

- **Use your flash in TTL mode.** Even when your camera is in Manual mode, TTL metering can still be useful for automatically and accurately managing the flash output for you. This means that TTL will do its best to properly expose your subject based on the manual settings you're using.
- **Use the highest ISO possible without introducing unacceptable noise.** You'll have to do some tests with your camera to see what your personal threshold is for noise. For some, an ISO of 800 is the limit, for others it might be 1600 or more. Many of today's dSLRs handle noise quite well so experiment with your camera to see what works for you. When you've found the highest ISO you're comfortable with for indoor photography, use it as a starting point each time.
- **Use the widest aperture that delivers acceptable sharpness.** Again, you'll have to determine what this is based on your lens(es). Budget lenses may not provide acceptable sharpness at their widest aperture, so you might find that on a lens capable of f/1.8, you're more comfortable with the images it produces starting at its f/4 setting. That will be your aperture baseline for that lens.
- **Start with the normal sync speed for your flash.** Some cameras automatically set flash sync speeds according to room lighting and/or camera mode. These will not always be the rated flash sync speed for the camera, but often a slower speed. In Manual mode you can make sure to set the shutter speed to the normal flash sync speed for your camera. The shutter speed setting is going to be your main control for creatively capturing and controlling the look of the ambient light in your images. Unless you're using High-Speed Sync, most of your creative shutter speed adjustments will be to speeds slower than the normal flash sync speed.

Strategies for Indoor Flash Photography

Once your settings are in place, the rest is about creative use of the camera, flash, and ambient light. Here are some strategies that will help bring out the best in your indoor flash photography:

Bounce Your Flash

If you can tilt and rotate your flash head, and you have light-colored walls, ceilings, and other large semi-reflective surfaces to work with, bounce the light from your flash for bigger illumination and softer light.

Use a Bounce Card for Dynamic Environments and Moving Subjects

Since you can't rely on always having a nearby light-colored wall to bounce your flash against, a bounce card will give you a little more flash coverage than direct flash, and you'll benefit from some added bounce off the ceiling, too.

Slower Shutter Speeds for More Ambient Light

If you're getting good flash exposures of your subject but you'd like to have a little more warmth or ambient light appear in the shots, just slip your shutter speed dial down to 1/60. If you'd like more, try 1/40 or 1/15. By simply adjusting your shutter speed dial up or down, you'll be able to control the appearance of the ambient light in the environment. Just remember that slower shutter speeds also raise the potential for noticeable blur or image "ghosting," which may or may not be a desired effect. Check your LCD monitor closely to judge if you're working within an acceptable shutter speed range.

Use FEC to Adjust Flash Power

Even though you're relying on TTL to control flash output automatically, you can still dial in more or less flash when a shot calls for it. Flash Exposure Compensation (FEC) allows you to override TTL if you need to make any adjustments on the amount of light you're getting from the flash. You won't need to use FEC often, but if your subject is wearing light colors, you might have to dial the FEC up a bit; otherwise, TTL might underexpose the shot. If your subject is wearing dark colors, you might have to dial the FEC down to compensate if TTL is overexposing the shot. TTL controls the flash output based on what it *thinks* is the best exposure, so sometimes you have to force it to accept more or less light from your flash to get things to look right.

Use a CTO Gel/Filter to Match Flash to Tungsten

If you notice that much of the ambient light is tungsten (e.g., household light bulbs), and there is an obvious or undesired mismatch between the flash illumination and the ambient light, you can attach a Color Temperature Orange (CTO) gel or CTO-colored diffuser over your flash to match the flash color to the ambient. Adjust the camera's WB setting to Tungsten, or leave it alone and adjust the WB with photo-editing software later (best when shooting to RAW format). Since the flash and tungsten lighting will closely match in color when using the correct flash filter, any WB adjustments to the image will affect all light sources evenly.

Indoor On-Camera Flash Techniques

Much of the flash photography you'll be doing indoors will be with the flash unit mounted on the camera and in TTL mode. The following techniques show you how to position and modify your flash to create better pictures with on-camera flash.

Direct, Forward-Facing Flash

As stated in Chapter 3, this is the most straightforward way to use your camera-mounted flash, but it can also result in unappealing lighting and shadows. Light coming directly from the camera's point of view (and the viewer's) doesn't provide the type of shadow information that gives a good sense of modeling or depth to the objects or people in the image. The most prevalent shadows tend to be the point-and-shoot variety that are cast just behind the subject. The effect of light drop-off is maximized in the image as it moves linearly from the subject to objects in the background. Illumination levels fall quickly as distance increases from the flash on the camera to the objects in the scene, then the background. This creates an unnatural look and contrast pattern in these types of images, as shown in Figure 4.1.

With that said, this in-your-face type of lighting has its place and doesn't have to be completely avoided. Also, by positioning your subject either right up against a background or wall, or a good distance from a darker background, you can avoid the type of background shadow that seems to define this technique's "amateur" feel.

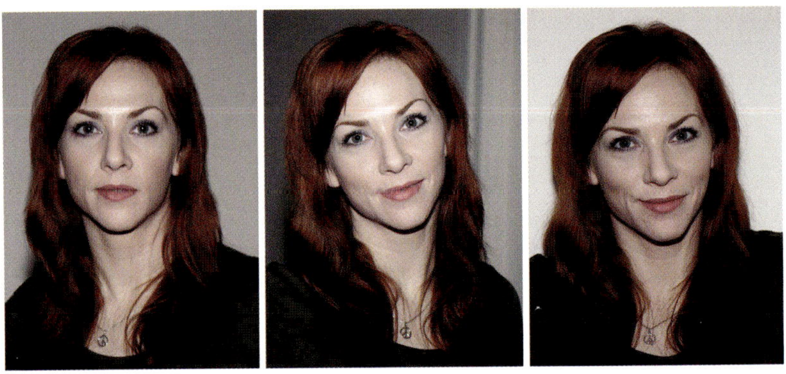

Figure 4.1 Direct, forward-facing flash examples shown at varying distances to the background.

Bounce Card, Horizontal and Vertical

One of the reasons on-camera, forward-facing flash has a harsh, in-your-face look is because the light coming from the flash is only a few inches above the camera lens. Gear and techniques that put more distance between the lens and the light emitted from the flash tend to provide more pleasing light and natural-looking shadows. With on-camera flash, a higher flash position (relative to the lens) gives a more pleasing illumination pattern on your subject.

A bounce card effectively creates a higher light source because it extends off the top of the flash reflecting light back to your subject from a higher angle. In this configuration, light from the flash is also directed at the ceiling creating an even higher, more diffuse source of light there. When the camera is held in the vertical framing positing (on its side), the flash head should be adjusted to point up at the ceiling again. Not only does this maintain a desirable ceiling bounce, but the configuration of the flash and bounce card gives your subject illumination from an angle slightly higher than the lens. This reduces the less attractive "side flash" lighting associated with on-camera flash when shooting with the camera in vertical orientation (see Figure 4.2). You can attach a bounce card made of flexible material, such as craft foam, to a flash head with a tilt/rotate feature by following these steps:

1. With the flash mounted on the camera in the normal, straight-ahead position, hold your camera the way you normally would for shooting vertically framed shots.

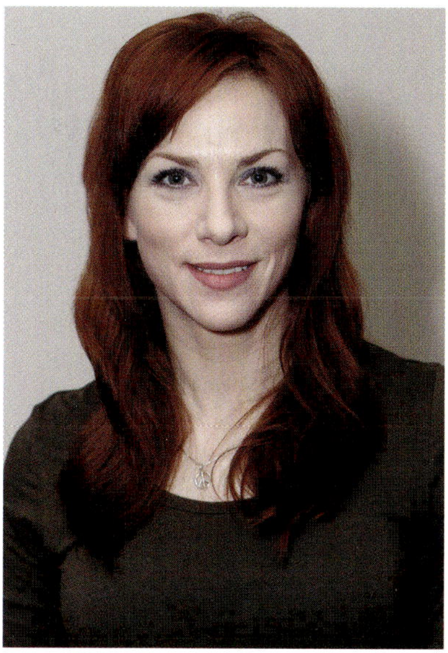

Figure 4.2
Using a bounce card creates a slightly higher and larger light source. Notice in this vertical shot, since the bounce card is above and to the left of the lens, the shadow on the wall has soft edges and falls down and to the right.

2. Press the Tilt/Rotate release and rotate the flash head so that it is pointing up toward the ceiling. (You will probably need both hands for this step, so rest your camera in your lap, on a table, or some other support.)
3. Wrap a rubber band around the flash head with enough tension to securely hold the bounce card in place.
4. Pull back the rubber band so that you can slide the bounce card between it and the flash head. Wrap the narrow end of the bounce card around the flash head so that the surface of the bounce card "opens" out in the same direction that the camera lens is pointing.

The bounce card is now ready to use. Simply press the Tilt/Rotate release button and tilt the flash head to always point up, whether you're taking pictures in vertical or horizontal orientation.

Wall and Ceiling Bounce

Using a light-colored wall/ceiling combination, you can fill much of the room with scattered, soft light. This is where a flash with a tilt/rotate feature becomes most useful. Follow these steps for basic wall/ceiling bounce with your on-camera flash:

1. Position yourself *at least* 3–4 feet away from the wall behind you with your subject in front of you at a normal distance (about 5'–7').
2. Tilt and rotate the flash head so it is pointing behind you about 45 degrees up toward where the wall meets the ceiling.
3. Take the photos as you normally would and adjust the angle of the flash for variety. For example, try side bounce (against walls to the side of the subject).

Aiming the flash behind you will send the light in that direction, where it will bounce off the wall and ceiling, creating a much larger and diffuse illumination for your subject. If you maintain the orientation of the flash to the wall, while you and/or your subject vary your positions, side lighting effects can be created (see Figure 4.3). As suggested in the steps above, you can also vary the angle of the flash to create more lighting variety. Be careful not to point your flash directly behind you at the wall. The light will bounce straight back to the front, with you in between the reflected light and your subject, casting your shadow onto her.

Mixing Ambient Light with Flash

Tungsten lighting in your background can add warmth, interest, and a sense of atmosphere to your images. While using flash, you can maintain full control over the effect of ambient lighting in your shots via the shutter speed

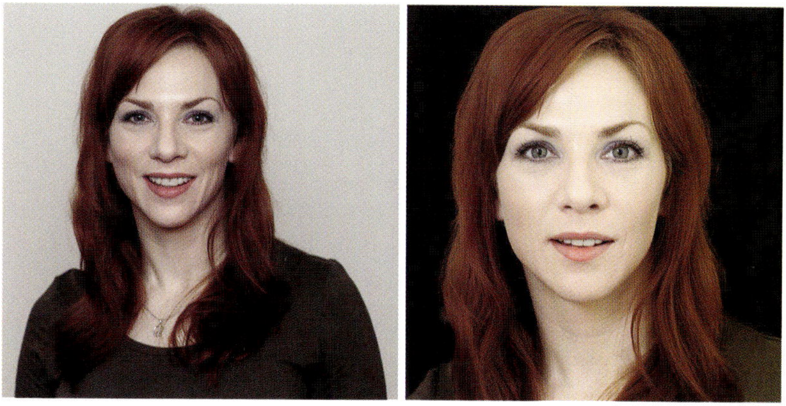

Figure 4.3 Bouncing the flash illumination off the wall in front of your subject will produce large, softer light (left). In a small room or corridor with light-colored walls, bounce lighting can result in very pleasing portraits (right).

(see Figure 4.4). In certain shooting modes, with your flash in TTL mode, your camera may automatically adjust exposure settings to help capture a good amount of ambient light. But by working in your camera's Manual mode, you'll have more control over the look of the room lighting in your images, while allowing TTL to handle the flash output to provide proper exposure for your subject. Follow these steps to get the desired amount of ambient light to show up in your flash photos:

1. Set your camera to Manual mode and your flash to TTL.
2. Use your preferred "starter settings" for indoor flash. An example of this might be:

   ISO: 800
   Aperture: f/4.0
   Shutter Speed: 1/250 sec. (or normal flash sync speed)
3. Take a test shot of the subject in your scene and note how the ambient light appears in the shot.
4. If you want the ambient light to appear brighter, lower your shutter speed to about 1/60, or 1/40. Remember that if you use slower shutter speeds, and there is any camera movement, or movement in the scene, there may be noticeable blurring or ghosting in the image. This is sometimes an acceptable or intentional effect.
5. If you want the ambient light to appear dimmer while using the normal sync speed, lower your ISO (to 400 in the case of this example) and/or close your aperture down a stop or two (try f/5.6 or f/8.0).

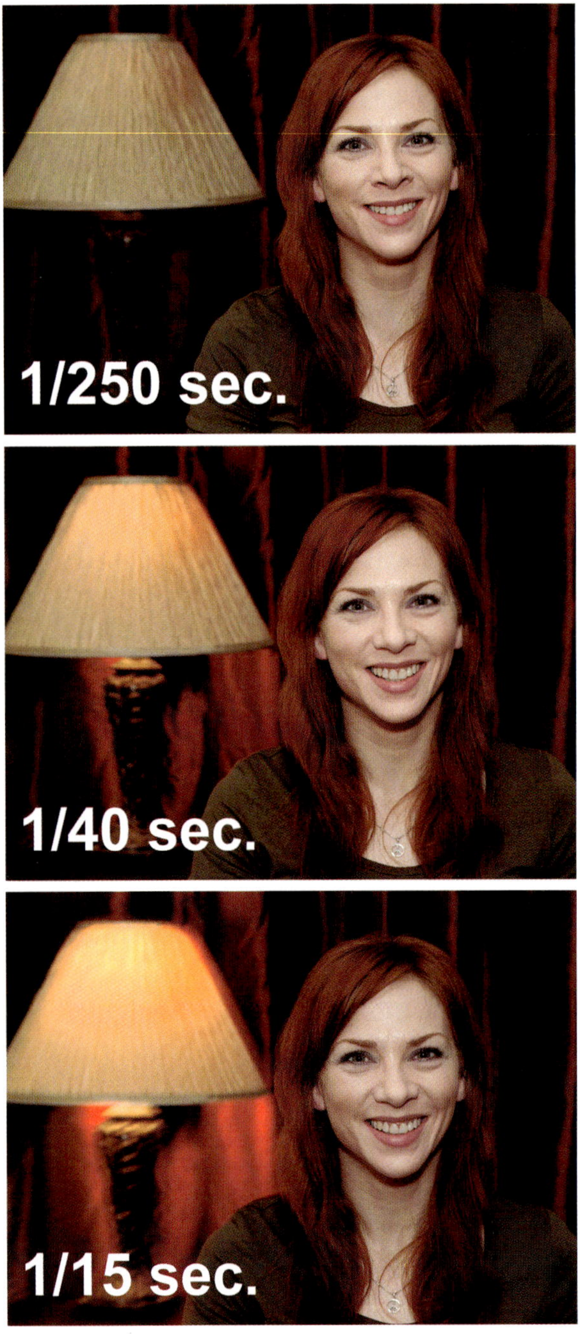

Figure 4.4
Here, the flash exposure, table lamp intensity, ISO, and f/stop were constant. Only the shutter speed was adjusted between exposures which brought in more of the ambient (lamp) light, but also resulted in some movement blur.

Using a CTO Gel to Balance Ambient and Flash Color Temperatures

Flash gels/filters allow you to change the color of the light emitted from your flash so that it is in the same color temperature range as most of the ambient light (see Figure 4.5). Indoors, the ambient lighting is usually in the warmer, tungsten range. With a CTO gel on your flash, it in effect becomes a tungsten-colored light, too. The entire image can be white balanced for tungsten as a whole, resulting in truer whites and other colors in the image. Follow these steps to properly use a CTO color-correcting flash gel:

1. Set your camera's WB setting to Tungsten.
2. Secure the CTO gel to the flash so that it covers the flash emitter lens. If your flash has an orange filter attachment, you can try using that instead.
3. Take images as usual. If there is still a slightly noticeable color cast it can be fixed in your RAW conversion or JPEG photo-editing software by reducing the orange/red hues, or adding some blue.

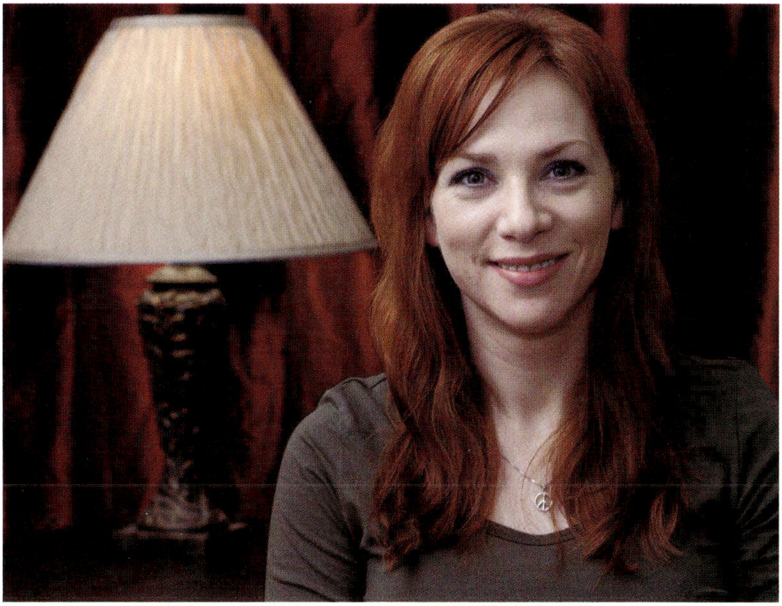

Figure 4.5 A CTO gel over the flash allows you to match the light emitted by the flash to tungsten light sources like the lamp shown here. With your camera WB setting on Tungsten, the orange cast created by the lamp, and color-filtered flash, is offset to produce truer whites.

Basic Portraiture Lighting

In the next section, we'll discuss off-camera lighting. But before going into the details of using your flash units in off-camera setups, it will be helpful for you to get a basic understanding of how positioning your flashes can greatly affect the look of your subjects. You already know that bounced flash can provide more pleasing illumination for your subject than when the flash is striking her directly from the same position as the camera. When your flash is taken off the camera axis your options for directional control of the light are almost limitless. Where you place your flash in relation to your subject can affect the look of the environment as well as the appearance of your subject's physical characteristics. With that in mind, we'll now introduce the five classic portrait lighting patterns which will help you make informed choices about how to position your main light with off-camera flash setups. These patterns can be applied to any lighting setup, including the ones described later in this chapter. Note that in the following examples, a single light is used, without fill lighting, in order to clearly show the effect of the main light.

Short Lighting

Short lighting is sometimes used as a corrective technique to help narrow the look of rounder faces. With short lighting, the main light illuminates the subject on the shorter side of the face, where the distance seems shorter from nose to ear (or nose to the edge of the cheek), from the camera's perspective. Another way to think about this is that when the subject has her head turned to one side, you are lighting the side of the face that is farthest from the camera, as shown in Figure 4.6.

When viewing a portrait, our attention is first given to the details we can see and to the brightest parts of the picture. Shadows recede and brighter areas are predominant. On a two-dimensional plane, there is actually less surface area visible on the side of the face turned away from the camera. With short lighting, this is the area that is highlighted with illumination from the main light source. Since more attention is given to the narrower surface area, a visual illusion is created that makes the subject's face look thinner. To create the short lighting pattern follow these steps:

1. Position your flash to one side of the camera, and higher than the subject's eye level. A good starting point is about 45 degrees off the camera axis and pointed down at the subject from a point slightly higher than her head.
2. Have your subject sit or stand with her shoulders at an angle toward the direction of the light source.
3. To complete the lighting pattern, your subject will turn her face about halfway toward the light source.

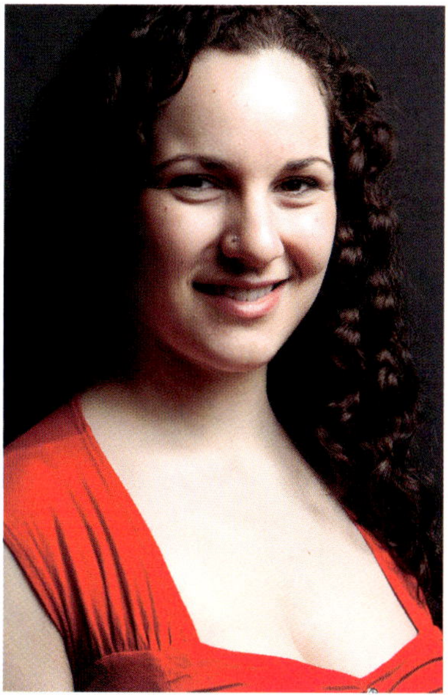

Figure 4.6 Short lighting.

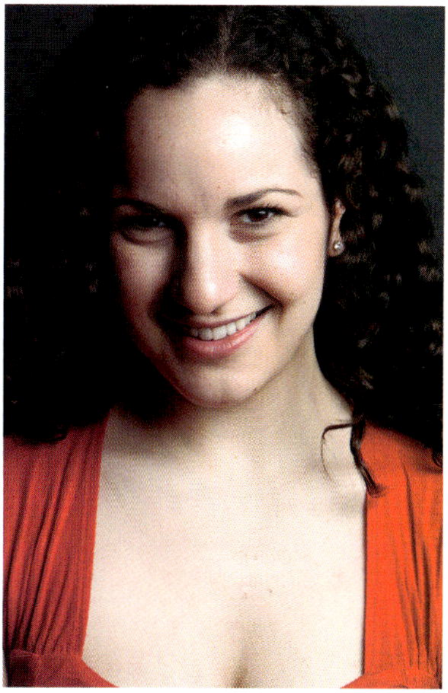

Figure 4.7 Broad lighting.

Broad Lighting

Here, the main light illuminates the subject on the broadest area of the face, from the camera's perspective. Another way to think about this is that when the subject has her head turned to one side, you are lighting the side of the face that is closest to the camera (see Figure 4.7). As a flip-side to short lighting, broad lighting simply places visual emphasis on the area of the face turned toward the camera; the area more in-line with the camera axis.

On a two-dimensional plane, there is more surface area visible on the side of the face turned toward the camera, as opposed to away from the camera. With broad lighting, this is the area that is highlighted with illumination from the main light source. Since more attention is given to the larger surface area than the narrower one on the side of the face turned away from the camera, a visual illusion is created that makes the subject's face look wider.

To create the broad lighting pattern follow these steps:

1. Position your main light source to one side of the camera, and higher than the subject's eye level. A good starting point is about 45 degrees off the camera axis and pointed down at the subject from a point slightly higher than her head.

2. Have your subject sit or stand with her shoulders at any orientation to the light source.
3. To complete the lighting pattern, your subject will turn her face somewhat away from the light source. When the light source is to the right side of the camera, the subject will turn her head so that the left side of her face is closest to the camera axis. Reverse the pose if the light source is on the opposite side.

Rembrandt Lighting

This lighting pattern, named after the Old Master painter, has a very classical look. The main light is positioned high and to one side of the subject creating a shadow from the nose that meets with the shadow from the side of the face opposite the light. The generally recognized definition of Rembrandt lighting where photography is concerned prescribes the use of the main light on one side of the subject's face in just the right position as to create a triangle or diamond shape of light on the shadow side just underneath the eye, to extend down toward the mouth.

To create the Rembrandt lighting pattern, similar to the one shown in Figure 4.8, follow these steps:

1. Position your main light source to one side of the subject, and higher than the subject's head pointed down at a 45-degree angle.
2. You must orient your subject's face properly in relation to the angle of the light to correctly execute this lighting pattern. The slightest rotation of her head will make or break the pattern.
3. Sitting, standing, or any other body position is up to you as this style of lighting is defined primarily by the way light falls on the face.

Butterfly Lighting

This lighting pattern, also known as Paramount or Hollywood lighting is identified by the butterfly shaped shadow that appears directly beneath the subject's nose (see Figure 4.9). It's reminiscent of Old Hollywood glamour photos and can be very dramatic. The main light is placed in front of, and somewhat above, the subject in order to create this look. This technique is especially effective and dramatic on subjects with pronounced cheekbones. Since the light is coming in from high and in front of the face, shadows drop in under the cheekbones and the chin. This also tends to visually bring the front of the face forward, set the neck into shadow, and cause other areas of the visual space to be downplayed.

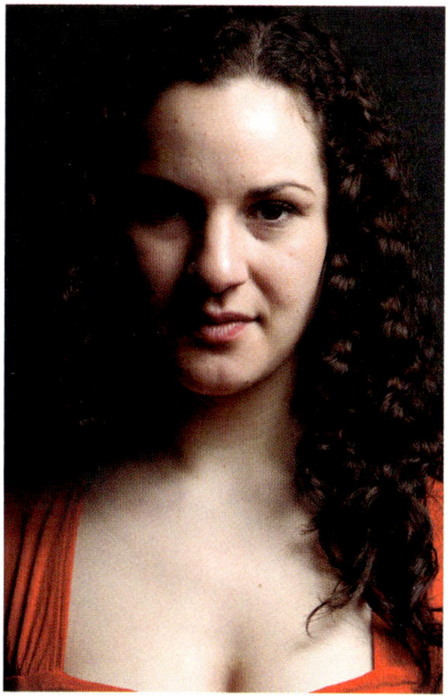

Figure 4.8 Rembrandt lighting.

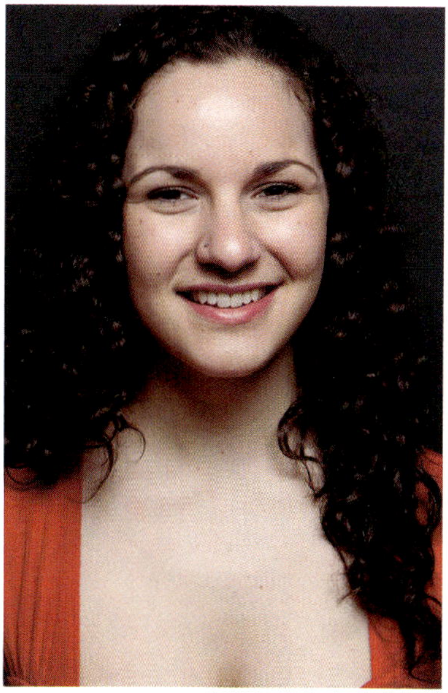

Figure 4.9 Butterfly lighting.

To create the Butterfly lighting pattern follow these steps:

1. Position your main light source directly in front of the subject's face, raised high enough over the head to create a symmetrical and small but conspicuous shadow under the nose.
2. Position the camera under the light source for a straight-ahead shot or to one side for a different view.
3. Since Butterfly lighting is defined by the shadow pattern created under the nose, the subject must maintain the angle of her face in relation to the light in order to properly execute it. As long as the nose-to-light position is held, you can vary your camera angle, and the subject can maintain eye contact with the camera, or look away, to create a variety of looks.

Split Lighting

Here, the main light is positioned to illuminate one side of the head while casting a full shadow on the other side (think of the center of the nose as marking the border). Split lighting visually divides your subject into light and dark areas of the image. If your subject is facing the camera directly when split lighting is employed, the face is likely to have a distinct shadow cutting vertically right down the center, as shown in Figure 4.10. The effect is rather dramatic and a

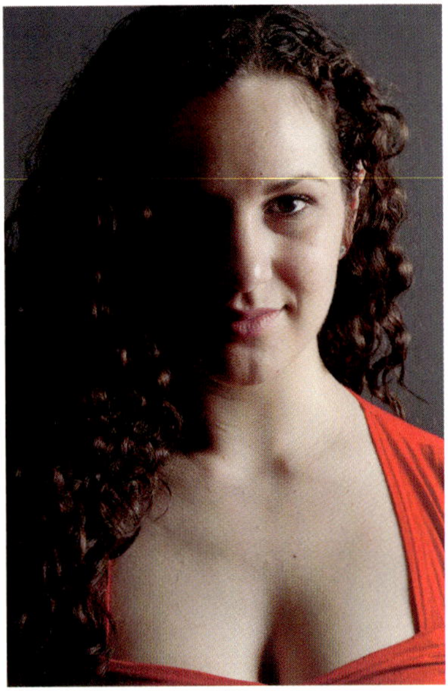

Figure 4.10
Split lighting.

low-key but high-contrast image is the typical result. Of course, you can change the amount or angle of the "split" by altering the position of the light or camera. Contrast can be adjusted, too, but as you increase the fill light, or widen your tonal range between light and shadow, you'll lessen the effect of the split. Split lighting is also a great way to bring out texture and detail, making this more appropriate for subjects with smooth skin, or when you'd like to really highlight the "character" in your subject's face.

To create the split lighting pattern follow these steps:

1. Place your light source directly to one side of your subject on a perpendicular plane to the camera axis. Increasing the actual or relative size of the light source will lower contrast; decreasing it will raise the contrast.
2. The only way split lighting makes sense is when there is something to split. With portraiture, the most effective use of this technique is when the subject is either directly, or almost directly, facing the camera.

Indoor Off-Camera Flash Techniques

Using your flash unit off-camera is always a nice alternative to on-camera flash. See Chapter 3 for details on the items you'll need and how to setup your off-camera flash units.

Flash Sync Cord with TTL

Nearby off-camera flash can be accomplished with a dedicated flash sync cord. These are usually rather short but still help you vary the directional quality of the light. These sync cords have dedicated contacts which allow you to use TTL as if the flash were still mounted directly to the camera. The TTL flash sync cord you use must be designed for your specific type of camera and flash. Two or more of these cords can be used together to extend the distance from camera to flash, although they are not necessarily designed to be used that way.

Using a Flash Sync Cord

Follow these steps to use a flash sync cord:

1. Attach and secure the "foot" connector of the flash sync cord to the hot shoe on the camera.
2. Attach and secure the "foot" of the flash to the shoe on the sync cord. The flash can be mounted on a bracket or held in your left hand. If you have a longer cable, or series of connected cables, the flash can be mounted to a light stand or some other support as needed.

A TTL flash sync cord is useful for capturing close-up and detail shots where you can vary the angle of light on the objects by simply holding the flash at different positions (see Figure 4.11). Unless it allows for at least 3'–4' separation from the camera however, it is only a slight upgrade from direct on-camera

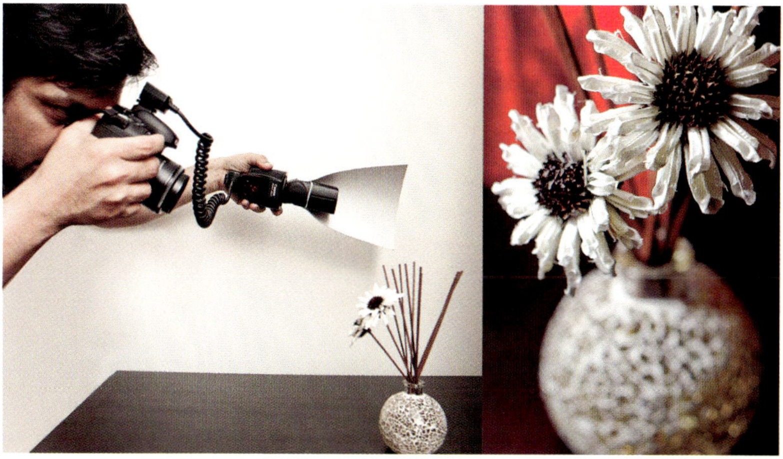

Figure 4.11 TTL sync cord and bounce card for controlling flash illumination on close-up objects.

flash when it comes to objects/people farther away from the camera. In that case, the flash will be too far for the photographer to hold it in his hand. It will have to be mounted to some type of extender, a stand, and/or held by an assistant.

Remote Flash with Wireless TTL

You can move the flash even farther from the camera when employing wireless TTL features. This frees you from the limitations of using a cord for camera-to-flash communication. It also allows you to use more than one off-camera flash unit. If your camera is equipped with a built-in TTL master controller or "commander" feature, you can use that; alternatively, a dedicated TTL wireless transmitter device or flash unit set to "master" will do the trick.

You'll have to mount your off-camera flash to a support, such as a light stand, or have someone hold it for you at the desired position and angle. Again, wireless TTL can be used successfully in most off-camera flash situations where the master controller can send and receive light signals to the remote unit(s). Indoors a direct line of site between master controller and each remote is not always necessary since the TTL control signals can be received by remote units as the signals bounce off the surroundings in the room. Outdoors, ambient lighting, distance, and other factors can more easily interfere with TTL light signal reception. Some newer products support radio transmitted TTL, which eliminates the problems associated with light signal transmittal. See Chapter 5 for more information on using off-camera flash outdoors.

Using Wireless TTL

Wireless flash needn't be complicated. Although you'll probably need to consult your camera or flash manual, you can follow these general steps to set up and use wireless TTL:

1. If using your camera's built-in master flash control feature, make sure your camera is set up as the master flash control. You might also have the option of disabling the built-in flash from contributing to the exposure (although it will send out a control flash pulse to the remote units).
2. If using a wireless TTL transmitter, or flash unit, mount it on your camera. A flash unit must be set to "master" in this case. You might also have the option of disabling the camera-mounted flash from contributing to the exposure (although it will send out a control flash pulse to the remote units).
3. The default settings are okay to get started with. There may be options for selecting different communication channels and flash groups, so be aware

that these must match up to your remote unit settings. Please see your manual for information on how to adjust flash output ratios and other advanced options.

4. Set your off-camera, TTL-compatible flash unit(s) to "remote" or "slave" mode. Again, make sure the settings on any remote flash units are either the default settings or they match up to the optional settings on the master unit or camera.
5. Position the off-camera flash unit to illuminate your subject and take a test shot. Determine if the light is creating the desired look on your subject and adjust the position of any remote flash units as necessary.
6. If the light is too bright or the subject appears over exposed because of the flash, use FEC to dial down the flash intensity. If the flash is not providing enough illumination to get a good exposure of your subject, use FEC to dial up the flash intensity.
7. Indoors, you can control the effect of ambient light as described in the previous section, "Mixing Ambient Light with Flash," just as you would if the flash were still on the camera. If the camera is in Manual mode, simply use slower shutter speeds to get more ambient light exposure in your images.

Non-TTL, Manual Off-Camera Flash

TTL often produces great results and provides you with a good amount of control over your flash output via FEC and lighting ratio control features. However, Manual flash control offers a more consistent and predictable flash output which can be useful at times. If you find that maintaining a specific flash power output is going to give you better results in a given situation, Manual flash is the way to go. Since Manual flash control does not require the use of TTL metering and output control—with Manual flash, you've pre-set your flash output power—all you need is a way to trigger the flash when you click the shutter. This can be accomplished via a standard sync cord, radio trigger, or possibly your system's wireless TTL features. Again, TTL metering is not involved, but your camera's built-in controller, a TTL transmitter, or master flash unit, may have the ability to send a signal to fire the remote flash unit(s) at the correct time.

You should also be aware that while your camera's various shooting modes are still available to you when using Manual flash, automatic flash output control is not available. It's to your advantage to use your camera's Manual mode when using Manual flash, if you want full control over the ambient and flash exposures.

Using Manual Off-Camera Flash Wirelessly

Follow these steps to set up and use manual off-camera flash wirelessly:

1. If using radio triggers, make sure the transmitter is connected to the camera and the remote receivers are connected to each remote flash unit. Continue to step 5.
2. If using your camera's built-in master flash control feature, make sure your camera is set up as the master flash control. You might also have the option of disabling the built-in flash from contributing to the exposure (although it will send out a control flash pulse to the remote units).
3. If using a wireless TTL transmitter, or flash unit, mount it on your camera. A flash unit must be set to "master" in this case. You might also have the option of disabling the camera-mounted flash from contributing to the exposure (although it will send out a control flash pulse to the remote units).
4. Set your off-camera compatible flash unit(s) to "remote" or "slave" mode.
5. The camera's shutter speed should be set to match the normal flash sync speed.
6. Set your remote flash units to Manual mode and start with an output setting of 1/8 power or less. An ISO of 100 or 200, and an aperture of f/4.0 or f/5.6 are examples of good starting points.
7. There may be options for selecting different communication channels, so be aware that these must match up to your remote unit settings (or your remote receiver settings if using radio transmitters).
8. Position the off-camera flash unit(s) to illuminate your subject and/or scene and take a test shot. Determine if the light is creating the desired look on your subject and adjust the position of any remote flash units as necessary.
9. If the light is too bright or the subject appears over exposed because of the flash, move the offending flash unit(s) farther away from the subject, use a lower flash output setting, a smaller aperture setting, a lower ISO setting, or combination of all of the above.
10. If the flash is not providing enough illumination to get a good exposure of your subject, move the flash closer (usually not closer than about 2.5') to your subject, use a higher flash output setting, a wider aperture setting, a higher ISO setting, or combination of all of the above.
11. Indoors, you can control the effect of ambient light as described in the previous section, "Mixing Ambient Light with Flash," just as you would if the flash were still on the camera. If the camera is in Manual mode, simply use slower shutter speeds to get more ambient light exposure in your images.

Using Manual Off-Camera Flash with a PC Sync Cord

In order to use a cord to sync the flash with the camera, both camera and flash must have some way to connect the cord—either through a built-in connector, or an adapter. This is often accomplished with a PC-type cord. One end of the PC cord is attached to the camera's PC terminal or adapter, and the other end is attached to a flash unit's PC connector or adapter. If multiple flash units are employed, the other flash units can be fired if they have optical slave triggers attached or built-in. In practical use, the idea is the same as with wireless triggering with the flash in Manual mode, except that there is a physical link between the camera and at least one flash unit. PC cord connections tend to be less reliable as the cords and connectors degrade and provide looser connections over time, so we do not recommend their use.

A note about optical slaves and triggering devices: Built-in or attached optical slaves, designed to trigger flash units when they see another burst of flash in the area, are useful in some situations, but not all. If you have tried to trigger external manual flashes by using your built-in or external TTL flash, you might have noticed your optically triggered units don't fire at the correct times. In fact, they are probably firing just before the actual exposure takes place, during the TTL pre-flash stage! There are workarounds to this problem, including special optical triggers/slaves that will take pre-flash into account during use. Keep in mind that optical slave devices may also fire their flash units if someone else is taking flash pictures nearby.

Example Lighting Setups

The following are examples of basic lighting setups that can be used with any type of lighting, whether it's constant illumination, shoe-mount flash, or studio strobe. The principles are the same no matter what type of light you use. However, since this *Compact Field Guide* is concerned with making expedient use of your flash, we'll discuss these setups with that in mind. We recommend mounting your flash units to light stands and using umbrella modifiers as described in Chapter 3. A good tip is to keep most of the light stand setups intact when not in use, so there is less to assemble whenever you pull them out for use. We also recommend setting your camera to Manual mode and off-camera flash unit(s) to TTL or Manual for the following setups:

One-Light Setup

If you have only one flash unit to work with, this setup is the obvious choice (see Figure 4.12). Using a single light, you can create each of the five portrait lighting patterns described earlier in this chapter. These setups will work with

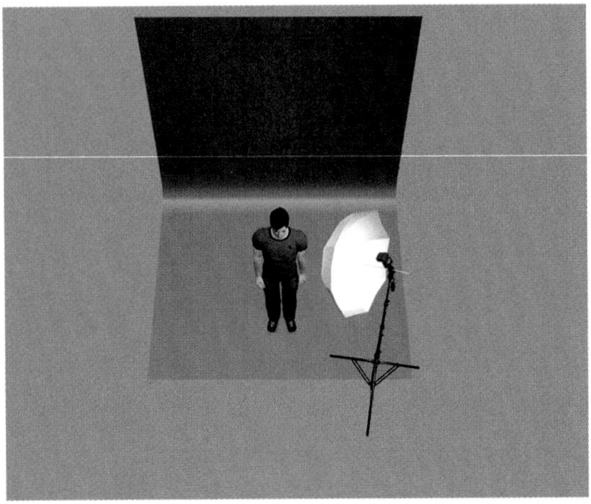

Figure 4.12
Diagram of a one-light setup. A flash unit is mounted on a light stand and modified with a translucent umbrella. It can be positioned either camera left (as shown) or camera right.

direct flash, but modifying your light can improve your results. In going with the principle that a larger light source will provide more even and diffuse illumination, we recommend that you place some type of modifier on your flash to get this effect; a photographic umbrella with translucent material is an easy-to-use, very effective choice. Simply position it on your light stand in the "shoot-through" configuration described in Chapter 3 and you're almost guaranteed excellent, studio-quality results!

1. Position your subject where you want them in the shot, taking into consideration the general angle and pose they'll start off with.
2. Position the light stand so that the closest part of the light source to your subject is approximately 2.5'–3.5' from their head as it's pointing directly at them.
3. Maintaining the subject-to-light distance, move the light to about 45 degrees off the subject-to-camera axis, either to the right or left of the subject.
4. Position the mid-point of the light or umbrella about 45 degrees up from the subject's eye line, so that the light is pointed down at them from slightly above their head.

This is a good starting point for most portraiture setups. As explained in the section on portrait lighting, you can vary the light, angle of the subject's head, and pose to achieve a variety of looks.

Two-Light Setup

Building on the one-light setup we move on to using two lights for even more creative options. It's helpful to think of any multiple-light setup in terms of each light having its own role to play. The two-light setup consists of a main light that provides the fundamental illumination of the subject, and a secondary light that can serve as fill, rim, or background lighting. When more than one light is being used, you'll find that balancing the output or intensity of the lights becomes important. Having each light illuminate the subject with the same intensity is not usually the goal, as you want to take advantage of the shadows provided by the main light to help model your subject. The secondary light serves an important role as it allows you to fill in the shadows or separate your subject from the background. Follow the one-light setup steps above for setting up the main light, then position a second light as shown in Figure 4.13 or Figure 4.14.

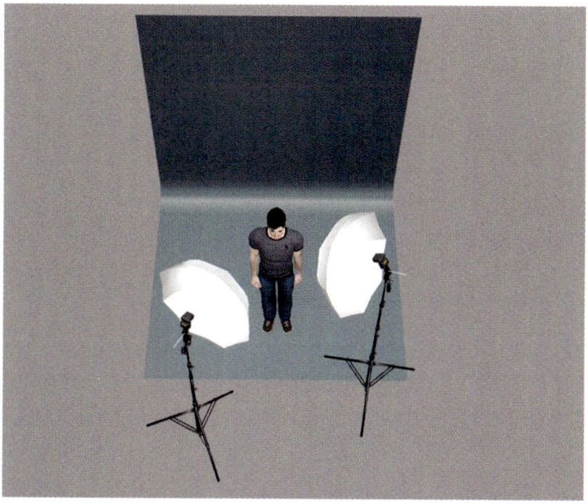

Figure 4.13
Diagram of a two-light setup, using second light as fill. One flash unit is positioned as described in the one-light setup above, while a second light is added to serve as a fill light on the shadow side of the subject.

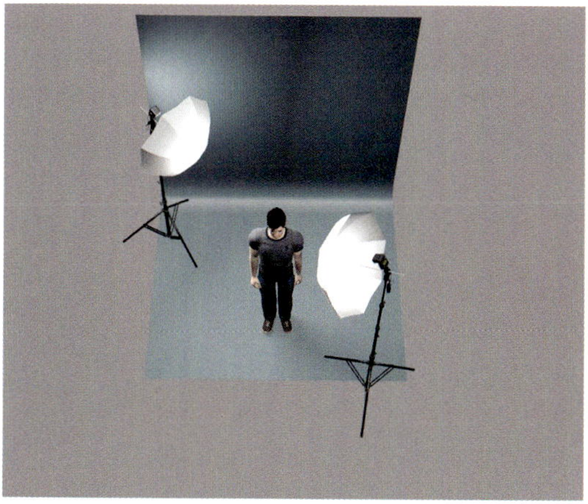

Figure 4.14
Diagram of a two-light setup, using second light as back/rim light. One flash unit is positioned as described in the one-light setup above, while a second light is added to create an outline highlight and background separation.

Using Three or More Lights

Having three or more lights available will further enhance your options. But as you increase the number of lights to your setup, it does become more complicated to manage. Again, it's helpful to think of each light as having its own role to play in the scene. The advantage of extra lights means that instead of having to choose what role your secondary light will play, you'll be able to have, for instance, your main light, one light providing fill, and a third to illuminate the background for effect. Building on the lighting setups above you can add a third light as shown in Figure 4.15, or even a fourth as in Figure 4.16.

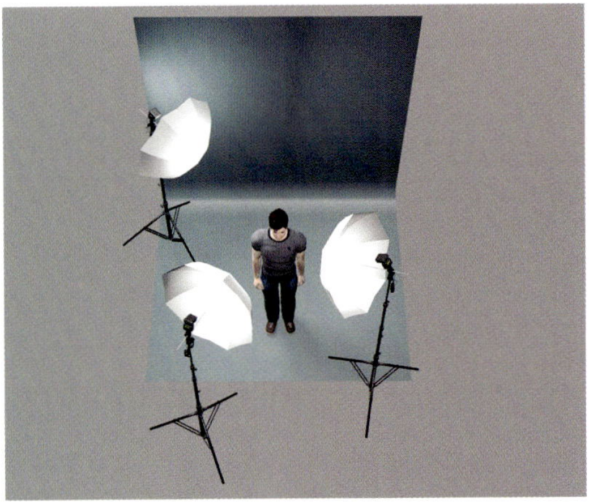

Figure 4.15
Diagram of a multiple-light setup. With the main light still in its original position, a fill light and a back/rim light are added.

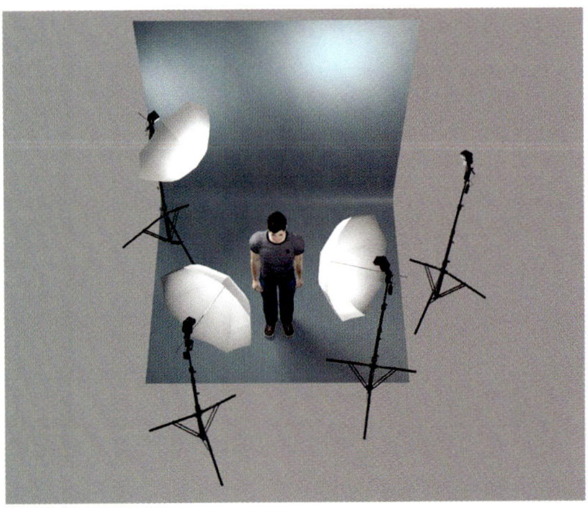

Figure 4.16
Diagram of a multiple-light setup. The original main light is supported by two modified lights (for fill and back/rim lighting) and an unmodified flash unit which serves as a background light.

Chapter 5

Outdoor Flash Photography

Outdoors, during daylight hours, one could make the argument that there is little need for flash illumination; all the light you need is already there. In contrast, flash is often the main light source indoors, being the brightest light in the room, if only for a millisecond. But flash plays a different role outdoors where the sun is your main light source. Here, flash generally serves as fill light, balancing illumination (see Figure 5.1), and less often, main light. In this section, we'll cover some important outdoor flash photography techniques.

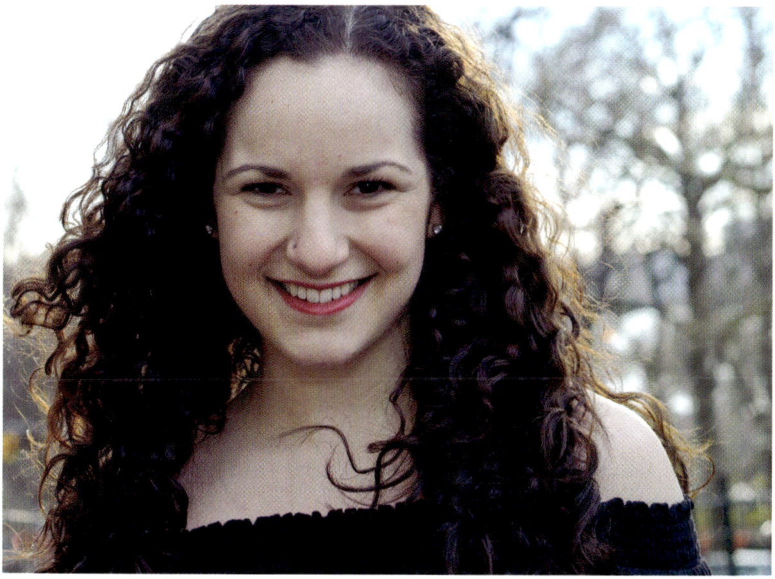

Figure 5.1 The subject is facing away from the sun which is providing all-around ambient light. A flash with an attached bounce card is being used with FEC set to –2 stops, providing natural-looking illumination for her face.

Initial Settings for Outdoor Flash Photography

We recommend that you adopt a regular starting point for your settings and controls. A standardized approach will give you the confidence of knowing exactly where you should start every time you use flash outdoors.

- **Use Aperture Priority for creative control.** For outdoor photography, especially where portraits are concerned, depth-of-field (DOF) is a major creative consideration. DOF is, of course, directly linked to your aperture setting, which you fully control when the camera is in Aperture Priority mode. In this mode the camera automatically adjusts the shutter speed according to the lighting conditions in the scene, and the aperture you select. If necessary, you can override the shutter speed selected by the camera using Exposure Compensation (EC) when in Aperture Priority mode. Note that with some camera and flash systems, adjusting EC will force an adjustment to flash output in the same direction. If this is the case, and you'd like to maintain the current flash output when adjusting EC, you'll have to make another adjustment to FEC in the opposite direction to compensate. Check your manual to see if this is the case with your system.
- **Use your flash in TTL mode with High-Speed Sync enabled.** For cameras and flash units to work together properly, a flash sync speed must be observed. The sync speed is the highest allowed shutter speed when using flash with your camera. This is usually somewhere between 1/200 and 1/500 second, depending on your model.

  A problem arises outdoors and in other very bright ambient lighting conditions: a proper exposure will often require the camera's shutter speed to exceed the flash sync speed. For example, at a reasonable aperture, and the lowest ISO setting, the camera's metering system might determine a shutter speed of 1/1000 of a second as being necessary for a good exposure, well out of range of normal flash sync speed. A solution has come in the form of High-Speed Sync for flash, which is available in all high-end flash units, and many more reasonably priced strobes. Through the use of a series of flash pulses, resulting in a slightly lower intensity, but longer duration of output, the flash is able to provide illumination at any shutter speed.

  The High-Speed Sync option can usually be left enabled even when it's not needed as it will only be activated when the shutter speed exceeds the normal sync speed. Since the flash intensity will be lessened during High-Speed Sync, it would be advantageous if aperture, ISO, and the lighting conditions in the scene resulted in a shutter speed matching the camera's normal sync speed. This best-case scenario is not always possible, especially when using wider apertures for pleasing DOF in portraiture. High-Speed Sync is best used as an up close fill light tool.

- **Use a low ISO.** Because of the abundance of natural, ambient light outdoors, and the likelihood that wider apertures are going to be used in portraiture, lower ISO settings are recommended. Unnecessarily high ISO settings may result in extra noise, higher shutter speeds (exceeding normal flash sync), and require you to stop down your aperture, limiting your ability to creatively use shallow DOF. Adjust your ISO as necessary to compensate for brighter or dimmer lighting conditions while maintaining normal flash sync speed (if possible), and your aperture of choice.
- **Use a wide aperture.** You'll have to determine what the widest acceptable f/stop is for your lens(es). Budget lenses may not provide acceptable sharpness at their widest aperture, so you might find that on a lens capable of f/1.8, you're more comfortable with the images it produces starting at its f/2.8 or f/4 setting. That will be your aperture baseline for that lens.

Strategies for Outdoor Flash Photography

Outdoor and indoor flash photography benefit from many of the same strategies. However, in daylight, flash is not always the best, or only, choice for illumination. There is after all, usually plenty of light for good exposures outdoors. Also, for nighttime photography outdoors, it might be difficult to locate a suitable surface to employ flash bounce techniques. With that said, here are some things that will help bring out the best in your outdoor flash photography:

Use Flash to Fill in Shadows

Sunlight provides the main light source for your outdoor images, but it will often cast heavy shadows and create harsh contrast. Using a flash to pop some light into those shadows is what fill lighting is all about. When used as a fill light, the flash produces just enough light to reduce and lighten the shadows and lower the contrast a bit.

Watch Your Shutter Speed

When shooting in the recommended Aperture Priority mode, shutter speed should be a secondary concern. Not because it's unimportant, but because the ambient light outdoors is usually strong enough to keep the shutter speed from falling into the range where blur is likely. However, in heavy shade, or low light conditions, your aperture and ISO combination might cause your shutter speed to drop to a point where camera shake or subject movement can cause blurring to occur. If you notice that your shutter speed is hovering in the lower ranges (e.g., 1/60 sec. or below), adjust your ISO to a higher setting and/or widen your aperture.

Use FEC to Adjust Flash Power

Even though you're relying on TTL to control flash output automatically, you can still dial in more or less flash output for the amount of fill light you want. Flash Exposure Compensation (FEC) allows you to override TTL if you need to make any adjustments on the amount of light you're getting from the flash (see Figure 5.2). TTL controls the flash output based on what it *thinks* is the best exposure, so sometimes you have to force it to accept more or less light from your flash to get things to look right.

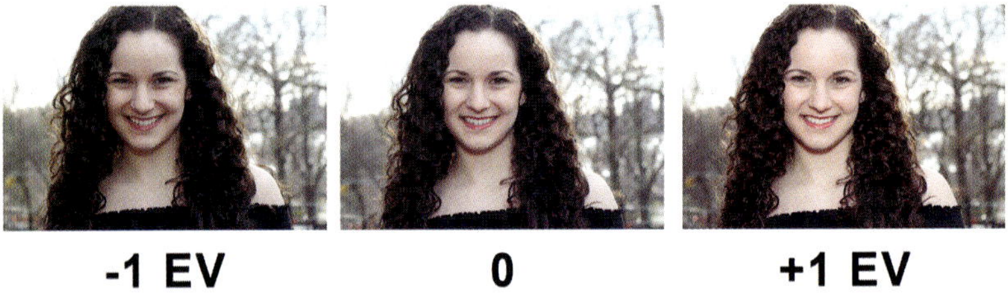

Figure 5.2 FEC can be adjusted for more or less flash exposure on your subject. This sequence shows the effect of FEC on flash output at –1 stop, 0, and +1 stop of compensation.

Use EC to Adjust Ambient Exposure

TTL and the flash affect the way the subject is exposed in the shot, but the flash can't illuminate most of the outdoor scene and background. The parts of the image well beyond your subject are, for all practical purposes, only being illuminated by the ambient light. Aperture, shutter speed, and ISO settings will all have an effect on how the ambient light appears in the image, whereas shutter speed normally has no effect on flash exposure. In Aperture Priority mode, adjusting the Exposure Compensation (EC) allows you to brighten or darken your background environment as shown in Figure 5.3. In this case, EC essentially lowers or raises the shutter speed, without changing the aperture.

As noted earlier, on some cameras, and in some setting configurations, adjusting EC also affects the flash output, which means that you'll have to take extra steps if you want to ensure the flash exposure remains constant when adjustments are made to EC. Check your camera's documentation to see if it allows EC and FEC to work independently of each other.

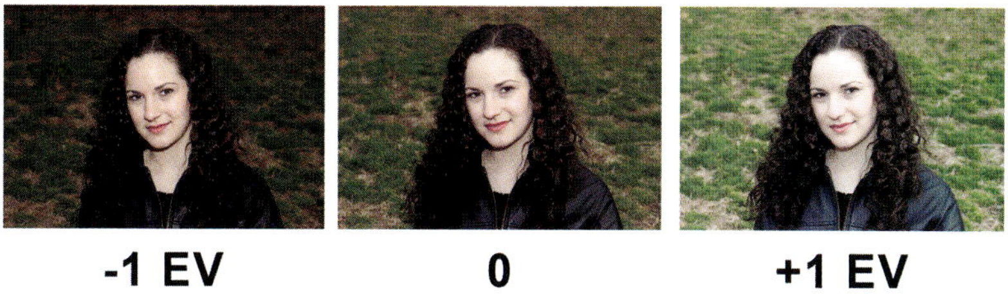

Figure 5.3 Exposure Compensation (EC) can be adjusted for more or less ambient exposure. This sequence shows the effect of EC on ambient light at –1 stop, 0, and +1 stop of compensation.

Outdoor On-Camera Flash Techniques

Much of the flash photography you'll be doing outdoors will be with the flash unit mounted on the camera and in TTL mode. The following techniques show you how to create better pictures outdoors with on-camera flash.

Flash as Fill Light

Using flash as fill light can give your outdoor images a more natural look. The idea here is to pop in just enough light to fill in the shadows and help reduce contrast (see Figure 5.4). Successfully applied, fill light can do its job without being too obvious. This way, it comes off looking like good natural light, instead of an artificial fix. Some cameras have very good automatic features that make it easy to produce good fill light. Whether you control your fill light manually, or let the camera work it out for you, the idea is the same: the overall

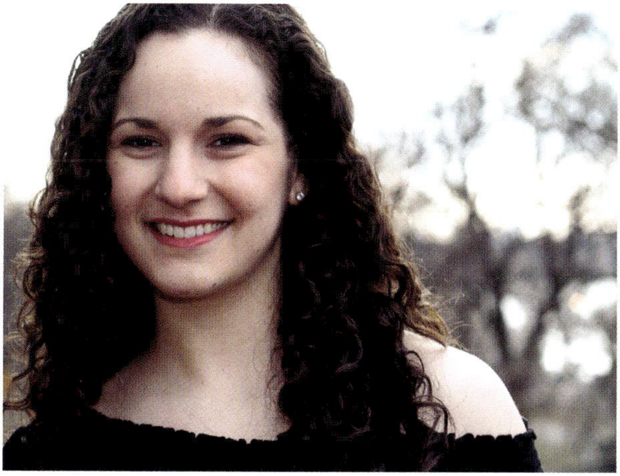

Figure 5.4 Using on-camera flash as fill light for outdoor daytime shots.

exposure of the scene is normal, and just enough light from the flash is emitted to create the desired effect.

Use the following controls to maintain good fill light:

- **In Aperture Priority or other camera modes, with flash in TTL mode:** simply dial flash power up or down using FEC. Your camera will let you know if this feature is not available for a particular mode.
- **With Flash in Manual mode:** dial flash power up or down as needed using the manual output control on the flash.

Flash as Main Light

It's possible to overpower morning or evening light, and even regular daylight, with your flash, essentially causing your flash to take on the role of the main light on your subject (see Figure 5.5). Depending on the ambient light levels, the flash may have to be used at, or near, full power to achieve this effect. The flash must be relatively close to the subject (whether you're using on- or off-camera flash) in order to achieve the proper light intensity on the subject.

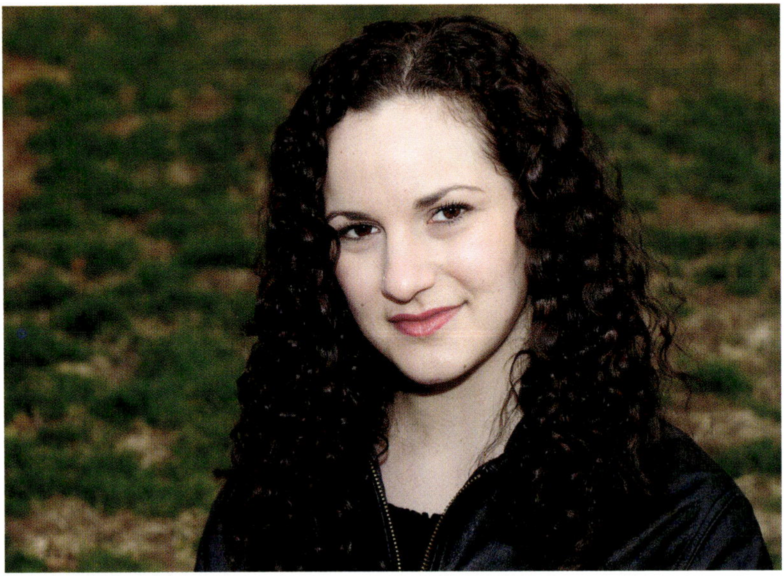

Figure 5.5 Using on-camera flash as the main light for outdoor daytime shots.

To use your flash as the main light:

- **In Aperture Priority, Shutter Priority, or Program mode, with flash in TTL mode:** Use Exposure Compensation (EC) to dial down the ambient light exposure by one or more stops as necessary. TTL-controlled flash will give the subject normal flash exposure. If your camera is set to adjust flash output along with EC, then you must compensate for that by using FEC to adjust the flash output back to normal exposure. For example: if you adjust EC by –2 EV and the flash output has been adjusted as well, the FEC should be set to +2 EV to make up the difference. Again, this is not necessary if the camera is adjusting EC independently of flash output. Test the EC feature out on your camera to see what modes it's available with.
- **In Manual mode, with flash in TTL mode:** Close your aperture down by a stop or two (e.g., if it's currently at f/4.0 set it to f/5.6 or f/8.0). This will darken the overall exposure, and TTL will force your flash to pump out more light on your subject to overcome the change. Of course, since it can't reach all the background areas, those remain darker.
- **In Manual mode, with flash also in Manual mode:** Note your camera's exposure meter. Underexpose the entire scene by closing the aperture down a stop or two (e.g., if it's currently at f/4.0, set it to f/5.6 or f/8.0). Your camera's exposure meter should read –1 EV or –2 EV (one to two stops underexposed). Now, adjust your flash power manually to achieve the amount of lighting you want on the subject.

Flash for Night Photography

Outdoors in dim light or darkness offers you few choices when it comes to creative lighting with on-camera flash, especially if there are no surfaces with which to use bounce flash. In order to give your images a sense of environment, you'll have to find areas of the background that are illuminated (see Figure 5.6). Use a bounce card to give your flash an added boost of surface area, and lower your shutter speed to help bring some of the ambient light into the exposure. As with indoor photography, your camera's Manual mode, coupled with TTL flash, is probably the best combination.

If you have additional flash units available, these can help pop some light into areas of the background. Off-camera flash with a single flash unit can also be used to create images with interesting light and shadow patterns. Use your creativity to add light to the darkness of night; car lights, store lights, and street lights can all add some atmosphere to the background which might otherwise just appear as a tunnel of darkness behind your flash-illuminated subject.

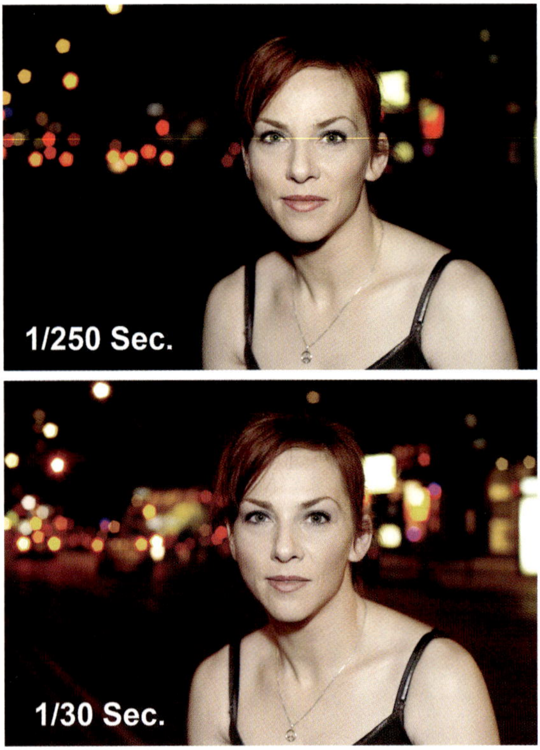

Figure 5.6
Night shots taken at shutter speeds of 1/250 second and 1/30 second showing how including more ambient light can help give a sense of environment to an otherwise dark scene. Even slower shutter speeds are possible if you mount your camera on a tripod.

Outdoor Off-Camera Flash Techniques

Using your flash unit off-camera is always a nice alternative to on-camera flash. Classic portrait lighting patterns as described in Chapter 4, might not be as easy to control in brighter outdoor conditions, but many of the same principles still apply. The environment can provide you with different light sources other than flash to accomplish many of the same things. For example, with a single flash setup, the ambient lighting can provide the main light, while sunlight coming in from slightly behind the subject or through the trees can provide a nice hair light, while your flash takes on the role of fill light. There are actually several ways to use off-camera flash successfully outdoors.

Flash Sync Cord with TTL

Nearby off-camera flash can be accomplished with a dedicated flash sync cord. These are usually rather short but still help you vary the directional quality of the light. These sync cords have dedicated contacts which allow you to use

TTL as if the flash were still mounted directly to the camera. The TTL flash sync cord you use must be designed for your specific type of camera and flash. Two or more of these cords can be used together to extend the distance from camera to flash, although they are not necessarily designed to be used that way.

Using a Flash Sync Cord

Follow these steps to use a flash sync cord:

1. Attach and secure the "foot" connector of the flash sync cord to the hot shoe on the camera.
2. Attach and secure the "foot" of the flash to the shoe on the sync cord.

   The Flash can be mounted on a bracket or held in your left hand. If you have a longer cable, or series of connected cables, the flash can be mounted to a light stand or some other support as needed.

A TTL flash sync cord is useful for capturing close-up and detail shots where you can vary the angle of light on the objects by simply holding the flash at different positions. Unless it allows for at least 3'–4' separation from the camera however, it is only a slight upgrade from direct on-camera flash when it comes to objects/people farther away from the camera. In that case, the flash will be too far away for the photographer to hold it in his hand. It will have to be mounted to some type of extender, a stand, and/or held by an assistant.

Remote Flash with TTL

You can move the flash even farther from the camera when employing wireless TTL features. This frees you from the limitations of using a cord for camera-to-flash communication. It also allows you to use more than one off-camera flash unit. If your camera is equipped with a built-in TTL master controller or "commander" feature, you can use that; alternatively, a dedicated TTL wireless transmitter device or flash unit set to "master" will do the trick.

You'll have to mount your off-camera flash to a support, such as a light stand, or have someone hold it for you at the desired position and angle as was done to create the image shown in Figure 5.7. Realize that outdoor conditions, like wind, can bring down your entire lighting setup, especially where large modifiers (e.g., umbrellas or softboxes) are used. Again, wireless TTL can be used successfully in most off-camera flash situations where the master controller can send and receive light signals to the remote unit(s). Outdoors, ambient lighting, distance, and other factors can easily interfere with TTL light signal reception. You may have to turn the body of any remote flash units so that the TTL light sensor points toward the camera (while keeping the flash head and light modifier pointed at the subject), assuming the flash offers this 180-degree

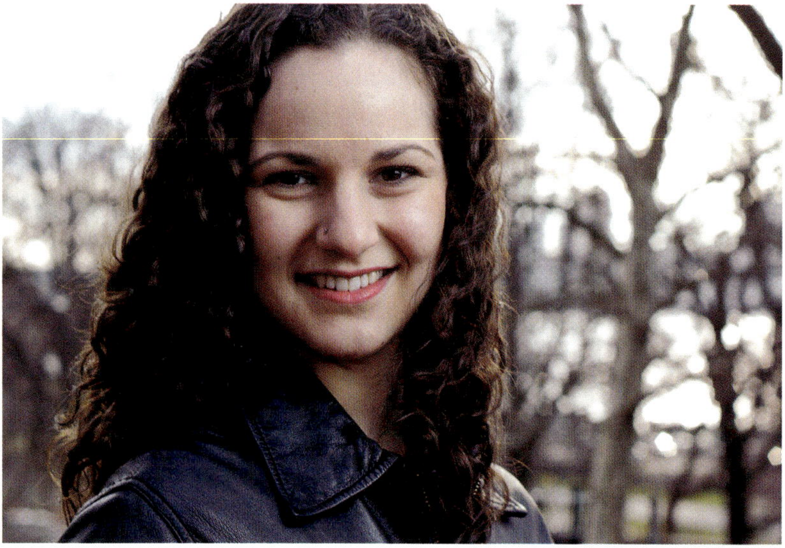

Figure 5.7 Using off-camera flash as the main light. This was taken with a 2' × 2' softbox designed for use with a shoe mount flash unit and held by an assistant at approximately 2.5 feet from the subject at camera right.

reversibility. It's recommended that you use wireless TTL at close distances when outdoors. Otherwise, radio triggering is probably a better option. Some newer products support radio transmitted TTL which eliminates the problems associated with light transmittal noted above.

Using Wireless TTL

Follow these steps to set up and use wireless TTL:

1. If using your camera's built-in master flash control feature, make sure your camera is set up as the master flash control. You might also have the option of disabling the built-in flash from contributing to the exposure (although it will send out a control flash pulse to the remote units).
2. If using a wireless TTL transmitter, or flash unit, mount it on your camera. A flash unit must be set to "master" in this case. You might also have the option of disabling the camera-mounted flash from contributing to the exposure (although it will send out a control flash pulse to the remote units).

3. The default settings are okay to get started with. There may be options for selecting different communication channels and flash groups, so be aware that these must match up to your remote unit settings. Please see your manual for information on how to adjust flash output ratios and other advanced options.
4. Set your off-camera, TTL-compatible flash unit(s) to "remote" or "slave" mode. Again, make sure the settings on any remote flash units are either the default settings or they match up to the optional settings on the master unit or camera.
5. Position the off-camera flash unit to illuminate your subject and take a test shot. Determine if the light is creating the desired look on your subject and adjust the position of any remote flash units as necessary.
6. If the light is too bright or the subject appears over exposed because of the flash, use FEC to dial down the flash intensity.
7. If the flash is not providing enough illumination to get a good exposure of your subject, use FEC to dial up the flash intensity.
8. Outdoors, you can control the effect of ambient light as described in Chapter 4 just as you would if the flash were still on the camera. If the camera is in Manual mode, simply use slower shutter speeds to get more ambient light exposure in your images.

Non-TTL, Manual Off-Camera Flash

TTL often produces great results and provides you with a good amount of control over your flash output via FEC and lighting ratio control features. However, Manual flash control offers a more consistent and predictable flash output. If you find that maintaining a specific flash power output is going to give you better results in a given situation, Manual flash is the way to go. Since Manual flash control does not require the use of TTL metering and output control—with Manual flash, you've pre-set your flash output power—all you need is a way to trigger the flash when you click the shutter. This can be accomplished via a standard sync cord, radio trigger, or possibly your system's wireless TTL features. Again, TTL metering is not involved, but your camera's built-in controller, a TTL transmitter, or master flash unit may have the ability to send a signal to fire the remote flash unit(s) at the correct time.

You should also be aware that while your camera's various shooting modes are still available to you when using Manual flash, automatic flash output control is not available. It's to your advantage to use your camera's Manual mode when using Manual flash, if you want full control over the ambient and flash exposures.

Using Manual Off-Camera Flash Wirelessly

Follow these steps to set up and use manual off-camera flash wirelessly:

1. If using radio triggers, make sure the transmitter is connected to the camera and the remote receivers are connected to each remote flash unit. Continue to step 5.
2. If using your camera's built-in master flash control feature, make sure your camera is set up as the master flash control. You might also have the option of disabling the built-in flash from contributing to the exposure (although it will send out a control flash pulse to the remote units).
3. If using a wireless TTL transmitter, or flash unit, mount it on your camera. A flash unit must be set to "master" in this case. You might also have the option of disabling the camera-mounted flash from contributing to the exposure (although it will send out a control flash pulse to the remote units).
4. Set your off-camera compatible flash unit(s) to "remote" or "slave" mode.
5. The camera's shutter speed should be set to match the normal flash sync speed.
6. Set your remote flash units to Manual mode and start with an output setting of 1/8 power or less. An ISO of 100 or 200, and an aperture of f/4.0 or f/5.6 are examples of good starting points.
7. There may be options for selecting different communication channels, so be aware that these must match up to your remote unit settings (or your remote receiver settings if using radio transmitters).
8. Position the off-camera flash unit(s) to illuminate your subject and/or scene and take a test shot. Determine if the light is creating the desired look on your subject and adjust the position of any remote flash units as necessary.
9. If the light is too bright or the subject appears over exposed because of the flash, move the offending flash unit(s) farther away from the subject, use a lower flash output setting, a smaller aperture setting, a lower ISO setting, or combination of all of the above.
10. If the flash is not providing enough illumination to get a good exposure of your subject, move the flash closer (usually not closer than about 2.5 feet) to your subject, use a higher flash output setting, a wider aperture setting, a higher ISO setting, or combination of all of the above.
11. Outdoors, you can control the effect of ambient light as described in Chapter 4, just as you would if the flash were still on the camera. If the camera is in Manual mode, simply use slower shutter speeds to get more ambient light exposure in your images.

Using Manual Off-Camera Flash with A Sync Cord

In order to use a cord to sync the flash with the camera, both camera and flash must have some way to connect the cord—either through a built-in connector or an adapter. This is often accomplished with a PC-type cord. One end of the PC cord is attached to the camera's PC terminal or adapter, and the other end is attached to a flash unit's PC connector or adapter. If multiple flash units are employed, the other flash units can be fired if they have optical slave triggers attached or built-in. In practical use, the idea is the same as with wireless triggering with the flash in Manual mode, except that there is a physical link between the camera and at least one flash unit. PC cord connections tend to be less reliable as the cords and connectors degrade and provide looser connections over time, so we do not recommend their use.

A note about optical slaves and triggering devices: Built-in or attached optical slaves, designed to trigger flash units when they see another burst of flash in the area, are useful in some situations, but not all. If you have tried to trigger external manual flashes by using your built-in or external TTL flash, you might have noticed your optically triggered units don't fire at the correct times. In fact, they are probably firing just before the actual exposure takes place, during the TTL pre-flash stage! There are workarounds to this problem, including special optical triggers/slaves that will take pre-flash into account during use. Keep in mind that optical slave devices may also fire their flash units if someone else is taking flash pictures nearby.

Chapter 6

Shooting Tips

In this book we've covered the most fundamental and effective ways to put flash to use in your photography. This chapter is designed to give you a quick overview of getting the most from using flash with specific subjects. Let's start with ten important tips to remember when shooting with flash:

10 Key Flash Tips to Remember

1. **Use flash only if it will improve your photos.** Just because you have a flash handy, doesn't mean it's necessarily the best light for the job. Much of the time, natural light, and some indoor lighting will provide adequate and pleasing illumination for your pictures. However, don't hesitate to use flash when lighting conditions call for it, or as a way to improve the look or usefulness of your images.
2. **Use TTL to keep it simple.** Through-The-Lens (TTL) flash metering is so useful there's every reason to have your flash set to TTL mode much of the time. TTL allows you to move freely and focus more of your attention on your subject, and less time fiddling with manual flash output settings. And even though TTL automatically controls flash output as you move about and change camera settings, it's still easy to make flash power adjustments via the Flash Exposure Compensation (FEC) dial. A great blend of automatic functionality and creative control!
3. **Bounce your flash.** This is probably the single-most important tip for using on-camera flash. Your flash is such a powerful tool; it can provide beautiful light without any extra gear or modifiers at all. Simply tilt and/or rotate the flash head so that the light emitted from the flash bounces off a large light-colored surface onto your subject.
4. **Bigger light is better light.** This fits right in with the bounce tip, but when you want a little more directional control over your light, use a modifier. Bounce cards, softboxes built for flash strobes, and umbrellas can really make a difference. Each of these will help create a larger surface

of illumination, which in turn, creates a softer and more pleasing light pattern.

5. **The closer the better.** The quality of your light has a lot to do with the relative size of the light where your subject is concerned. Bigger light provides more even and diffuse coverage. But even larger light sources don't work as well if they are farther away from the subject. You don't just sacrifice light intensity; you also lose the coverage it can provide if it were closer to the subject. Keep any sized light closer to your subject so that it covers as much surface area as possible.
6. **Apply fill flash in outdoor portraits.** Ambient and sunlight are the natural sources of illumination for your outdoor pictures. To keep your outdoor images looking natural, use your flash to fill in the harsh shadows often associated with bright sunlight. Some of the best outdoor pictures benefit from flash photography without looking like flash was even used.
7. **Move your flash off the camera.** Off-camera lighting provides you with options you just can't get with a single, on-camera flash. By moving your lights off the lens axis you are able to model your subject with more natural shadow patterns. This adds dimension and interest. When you employ off-camera lighting, the use of a light stand and a modifier can take your lighting to near studio-quality levels, plus it eliminates any chance of red-eye reflections which are sometimes possible even with external flash units Add more lights as you see fit.
8. **Always have fresh batteries on hand.** Flash units can drain your batteries quickly and running out of power before you're finished shooting is never fun. If you're using rechargeable batteries, make sure they're fully recharged and ready to go each time you set out to take photos.
9. **Make use of ambient light.** Flash and your camera settings can overpower and/or underexpose other lights in the environment. These lights (e.g., lamps, candles, etc.) can be important elements, providing atmosphere for your images. Rather than have one bright flash light the scene, you can dial down the shutter speed a bit to give the weaker ambient light a chance to make more of a showing in the exposure. If you're shooting at 1/250 sec., try 1/40 sec. or so and see how that does. Remember to watch for unwanted blur at slower shutter speeds.
10. **Use color-correcting gels and proper WB.** Color casts can give your images a cooler or warmer look than you would like and using the correct WB setting indoors might not solve the problem all by itself. Use a CTO gel over your flash to essentially have it produce a tungsten-colored light, rather than the cool light it normally emits. With the entire scene illuminated in warm tones, your WB Tungsten setting will give you more accurate colors overall.

Flash Photography for Specific Subjects

Here is a list of tips for some common flash photography subjects:

Portraiture

There are few things more captivating to us than the human face. In each other's faces we see emotion, feel a connection, read cues, and ultimately see ourselves. When you create a portrait, you capture a moment in time in someone's life; some say, their essence. And unlike images of objects or landscapes, portraits can create a sense of connection between subject and viewer so strong that even a simple snapshot can become a treasured keepsake.

In Chapter 4, we discussed the five basic portrait lighting techniques. Each of these techniques can be accomplished with a single flash unit to create compelling images. Bounce lighting can also be used to create beautiful portraits in a less formal way, where you and the subject can move freely in the environment. Adding more lights and reflectors can give you more creative options with some added, but often worthwhile, complexity.

Outdoor portraits benefit from wider apertures which allow you to creatively blur the background. Using flash for fill gives the subject of your portrait a little extra pop and helps fill in any heavy shadows. Indoor portraits can run the gamut from simple headshots with nondescript backgrounds to wide, environmental portraits that frame the subject together with their surroundings. Here are some tips for getting great portraits with your camera and flash units:

- **Use bounce flash indoors.** If you are not able to use off-camera flash and flash modifiers, use bounce flash to achieve soft, even illumination for your subject. If your flash unit has a tilt/rotate feature, you can simply use a light-colored wall and ceiling as a giant flash reflector. Rotate your flash head 180 degrees from the front, then tilt it 45 degrees up so that the light bounces off the wall behind you. If you're positioned about 4'–6' from the wall behind you, and your subject is a few feet in front of the camera, beautiful lighting is almost guaranteed!
- **Light from above.** We're wired to accept overhead illumination as more pleasing and natural. By positioning your flash to light your subject from a position above, and to the front of the head, you'll achieve a lighting pattern on the face that is more flattering than light striking your subject from below the eye line. With off-camera flash, this is possible by placing a flash and modifier (e.g., a translucent shoot-through umbrella) in the 45 degree up, and 45 degree off-axis position detailed in the portraiture lighting examples in Chapter 4. When using on-camera flash, a bounce card or some other method of raising the relative height of the light source will also help.

- **Use fill light to soften contrast and lighten shadows.** With indoor flash portraiture, any white, reflective surface or a second light positioned on the shadow side of your subject will help add some illumination to that side of the face. By placing your subject near a light-colored wall, you can easily use it as a reflector for a flash on the opposite side. Otherwise, something like a white piece of foam core, poster board, or even a square of fabric can help bounce some illumination off the main light onto your subject's shadow side. If you have a second flash, you can use it on the shadow side instead, to serve as the fill. Make sure that the fill light has either a lower output than the main light, or is positioned a little farther from the subject, so its intensity is less than that of the main. Outdoors, your flash is often going to be your fill light, as the sun and ambient light will play the role of main light(s).
- **Create background separation.** The subject of your portrait isn't the only thing the viewer will see in the picture; there is the background to consider. It's the way you present the subject against the background that creates a sense of depth and atmosphere to the overall image. One way to achieve this separation is to contrast the tones and colors of the background with the colors of the subject's hair and/or clothing. A problem can arise when those colors are too similar, or dark hair becomes indistinguishable from a dark background. If you notice the problem is the latter, you can use a second flash, or another light source (including ambient), to strike the subject from the opposite side of the main light. This should create a side/rear outline or highlight to that side of their hair and/or figure, creating a distinct separation. This technique can also be used to create a more subtle highlight to add extra dimension to a portrait as shown in Figure 6.1.

Sports and Action

Capturing sports poses a few logistical problems where flash photography is concerned. Many sporting events will preclude you from getting close enough to the action for your flash to have any real effect. From the average spectator position at an arena, for instance, there's no point in firing your on-camera flash at all. And if you manage to get a position on the sidelines or courtside, there are sometimes restrictions from using on-camera flash. Professional photographers will often get permission to mount flash lighting (as well as remote-controlled cameras) around the playing fields and indoor structures, but this isn't particularly necessary where good event lighting is provided. For much of sports, the modern dSLR, with its high ISO capabilities can gather enough light at higher shutter speeds, for good exposures. Of course, a "fast" lens capable of wider apertures is a must.

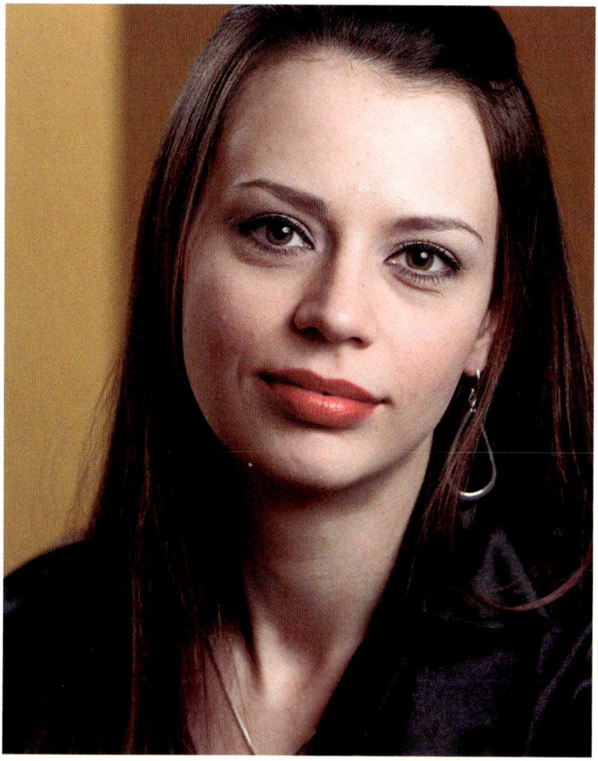

Figure 6.1
Notice a backlight serves as a subtle hair light for extra dimension and separation from the background.

High shutter speeds are what we're after with sports and anytime we want to freeze the action. But if you're not shooting in a well-lighted arena, or outdoor event, you might find that even the best digital camera can use a little help from your flash.

Here are some tips for using your flash photography to capture the action:

- **Ask permission.** Even if you know one of the participants or event staff personally, make sure you have permission (or otherwise know that it's acceptable) to take photographs during the event. If you are planning to use off-camera flash units, make sure you're cleared to mount them somewhere.
- **Get close to the action.** Whether you're shooting with a wide angle or telephoto lens, the closer you are able to get to the action the better. Get right up to the sidelines if possible and plant yourself there for a while. Wait for the action to come to you, anticipate the shot, and snap it. Being close and mobile helps you vary your angles and puts less load on an on-camera flash.

- **Don't overdo it with flash.** It can be very easy to get carried away and shoot a rapid sequence of shots when the action gets exciting, but slow it down. For one, your flash may not be able to recycle fast enough to keep up. For another, it might become very annoying to the other spectators and participants and you may be asked to stop shooting. Pace your shots, and try to capture that one good shot at a time, rather than shooting several frames to select from later.
- **Use your camera's manual mode.** Using manual mode will allow you to maintain complete control over your shutter speed, which is important anytime you want to capture your subject in motion. Use a high ISO and reasonably wide aperture to maximize the effect of your flash's output.
- **Use blur to your advantage.** Using a combination of blur and frozen action can really help tell the story. Panning and slower shutter speeds, together with rear-curtain sync, can help give you a clear view of the subject, as well as a controlled trail of his/her motion. It might take several attempts just to get one good shot like this, but it's worth the trouble when it results in a great action photo.

Interiors and Exteriors

There are times when spaces and structures become the subject of your photographs. This type of photography is useful for real estate, editorial, and many other purposes. But spaces and structures can pose a variety of challenges when it comes to photography. With basic camera gear there can be problems with lens/perspective distortion that either have to be addressed with special tilt-shift lenses or attachments or corrected with image-editing software. Where illumination is concerned, outdoor shots of exteriors during the day are almost entirely at the mercy of the sun's position in the sky and/or cloud conditions. The sun is your main light source and it will cast heavy or long shadows on a building at certain times of the day. At other times, the entire side of a building will be in shadow. So, it's important to photograph the structure at a time of day that minimizes those shadow patterns, if at all possible. Using a flash as fill for hard cast shadows on larger buildings is not usually going to be successful. On smaller structures where each part of the building facing the camera is going to be illuminated at equal distance to your flash, you will have more success.

Evening or nighttime exterior shots can also be successfully achieved without flash if the exterior lighting is balanced and even. Unfortunately, this is rarely the case as most of the illumination is usually accent lighting and light emanating from the interior through the windows. Long exposures are going to be necessary to capture the scene, and the areas with more light will often become overexposed in order to record the rest of the structure. Flash can be useful here if placed correctly but you'll have to experiment in order to get a desired result.

Interior photography can benefit a great deal from flash. As we've shown in this *Compact Field Guide*, simply bouncing your flash against one side of a room can create a broad, even, and beautiful illumination. Things, of course, get more complicated when the interior shots are to feature bigger spaces, partial views of closets, hallways, and other rooms, window light, and ambient lighting fixtures. Keep in mind that some interiors are designed to be darker rather than brightly illuminated (e.g., control rooms, production studios, bars, romantic restaurants) and a tripod and longer exposures may be more appropriate than introducing flash.

Here are tips for shooting interior spaces:

- **Balance color temperature where necessary.** While it may be acceptable for some of the ambient light to appear warm in tone as shown in Figure 6.2, large areas of color casts within a scene are often less desirable. When using flash, take a quick test shot of your scene, with all of the lights in the room on, and examine the LCD preview to spot color temperature problems. Solutions might include simply turning off some of the indoor illumination, replacing tungsten lights with daylight-balanced ones, or adding color temperature-correcting filters to your flash. Additional challenges may arise from painted or wall-papered surfaces that create noticeable color casts. Sometimes the best option is to color-correct with photo-editing software as was done with Figure 6.2.
- **Bounce light throughout the room.** Unless the environment is designed to be darker, fill it up with illumination for the camera. This is best accomplished with the light from your flash hitting and reflecting off of the large, light-colored surfaces in the room. Experiment with simple diffusion attachments that scatter light all around, basic wall/ceiling bounce, and large translucent shoot-through umbrellas to find the best light spread for the environment.
- **Watch for flash reflections.** The intense light of a flash will be very noticeable in certain reflective surfaces in a room. Mirrors, wall décor, windows, glass block walls, shiny furniture, and even kitchen appliances can all reflect specular light from a bright source like your flash, directly into your lens. Don't be surprised to see a ghost image of your lighting

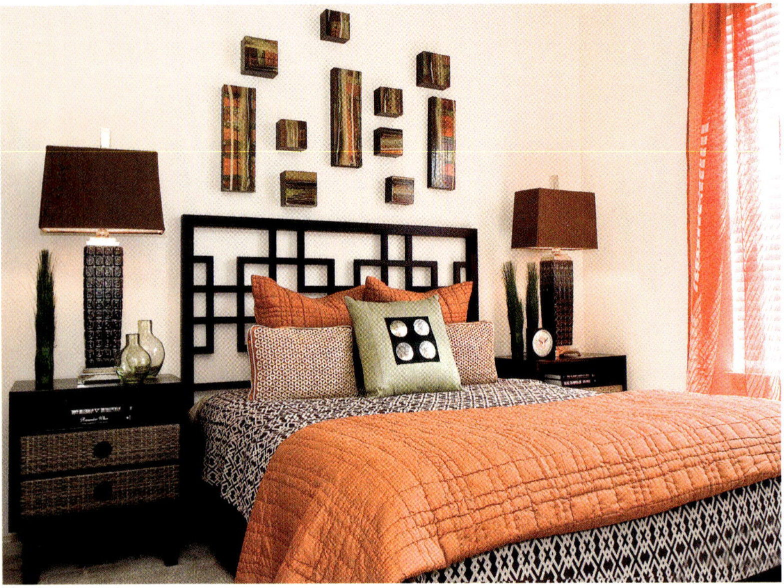

Figure 6.2 This scene contains daylight (window), flash lighting, and tungsten light emanating from the lamp. The tungsten has a slightly warm tone, but does not distract from the scene or create an undesirable color cast.

setup in a window which only became visible in your shot when the light flashed bright enough to cause a reflection. Just make sure to check your previews for any bright spots and gear reflections.

- **Use appropriate f/stops.** When the environment is your subject, you'll have to decide how much of it (if not all of it) should be in focus. If the focus is only part of the room, wider apertures are okay. But if you're trying to capture the look of the entire room, smaller apertures are going to be necessary, which means you'll have to either raise your ISO or increase flash power.
- **Use more than one light in larger environments.** Remember that the environment is essentially sculpted by the light you put into it. You will make parts of it recede into the background by allowing them to be darker. By adding light so that everything in the frame is well illuminated, it opens up the space. Still, a sense of separation and definition can be created by selectively lighting pockets of the scene. More lights in a larger environment give you these options.

- **Paint with light.** By taking advantage of the extended exposure times called for in nighttime photography, you can effectively illuminate large areas of an exterior evenly with a single flash unit. Mount your camera to a tripod and adjust your manual exposure and flash settings so that you will achieve a good flash exposure on any portion of your image illuminated by the flash. Using a low ISO, small aperture, and long shutter speed (30 seconds or more), trip the shutter. With flash in-hand, on a predetermined power setting, proceed to "paint" the structure with the light from the flash. Simply hold the flash at the same distance to each portion of the structure and fire it with the test button. When the shutter closes, the exposure is over. With some quick test shots and a little trial-and-error, this technique can be very effective for lighting exteriors as well as interiors.

Product and Detail Photography

Whether you're selling jewelry online or putting together a webpage for your pastry shop, good product photography can make your items more attractive and marketable. Product photography isn't simply a matter of pointing your camera at an object and snapping the shutter; it's about illustrating an item for the purposes of marketing. You'll want to give your viewers a clear sense of what your product looks like, and an idea of what it might feel like, too. Fortunately, with a simple understanding of flash photography and one or two basic flashes, you'll be able to create images that rival any professional product photography or catalog shots.

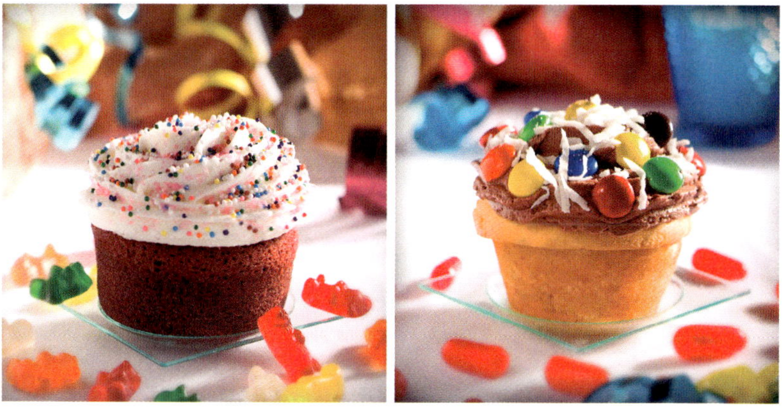

Figure 6.3 These food product shots were created with back/side lighting to bring out the texture in the cupcakes. Party favors and other items were positioned around the treats to make things look more festive.

Although there are plenty of product photography kits available, there is no single best way to shoot every type of item. Some items benefit from more even illumination, while others really pop with a little side/backlighting to enhance texture. Background is important, too. You don't want it to compete with the product on display, but rather help present it without distraction. (See Figure 6.3.)

Still life and detail photography are similar to product shots, but not always done for the purposes of marketing. Whether it's macro or small- to medium-sized objects, photographing objects close to the camera can give the viewer an opportunity to appreciate them in photos and often with a different perspective than is possible with their own eyes.

- **Bring out the detail and texture.** Naturally, you want to make sure your product has good illumination on the camera side so it is clearly visible in the image. But by lighting your item from the side and slightly behind, you can create more contrast and definition in the details and textures. If necessary, snoot your flash so that the light is focused hard on an area of the product to achieve this effect. Holding your flash just to the side or above a smaller object can also create interesting detail lighting. This is not only a great strategy for food photography, but also for anytime you want to give the viewer a tactile sense of an object. Your choice of aperture will be important, too. Use smaller apertures that capture all of the product's detail, but wide enough so that your lighting can still produce proper exposures.
- **Choose the right background tones.** White backgrounds are commonly used because they are light and void of any distracting visual information. Where a sense of space is desired, a graduated background is sometimes created. This is often accomplished with a feathering of the light so that the background is lighter near the item being photographed, and darker as the background recedes. Sometimes, a bold color, or simple black is used to help make the product look more exciting, playful, or important. If using very dark colors, be sure you define the edges of the item with your flash or a reflector so that it does not disappear partially into the darkness.
- **Use reflectors for fill light.** Having multiple flash units on hand can really make a difference in product photography, but there are ways to illuminate your items from multiple angles even if you only have one or two flash units on hand. Small mirrors, aluminum foil, white foam core, and even typing paper positioned close to an object being photographed can be used to reflect a good amount of light onto one or more sides of the

item. If you set up your product shots on a table close to a white wall, you can angle the flash to come in on one side, allowing the wall to act as your reflector on the other. You'll have to experiment and take test shots to make sure you're getting the fill and reflections you want, but where product photography is concerned, there are no hard rules for lighting. Getting it right is often a matter of trial-and-error.

- **Stay consistent.** Most product photography doesn't involve just one image, or a single product; make sure all of the images in a set are similar in terms of lighting and framing. This will make things appear more uniform and professional to the viewer. Make sure you take notes so that you can consistently re-create the same lighting in future product shots. Some things that can help you maintain consistency include using a tripod to keep the camera and setups in the same position throughout a set of images, and carefully placing each new object to be photographed in the same spot on the display area.
- **Use other objects and background for context.** Sometimes an object or item can benefit from having additional elements in the shot. A good use of depth-of-field will help you ensure the background is not too distracting, yet still provides a sense of atmosphere. Elements that give the main object a sense of purpose, dimension, and context can help tell the story, too. Up-close flash might not be as good a choice with this type of shot as it will tend to light a very small area, leaving the background and nearby objects in the dark. Use bounce or off-camera flash (multiple and/or reflectors) for the best results.

Music and Stage

Indoor events, regardless of the available lighting, often require a little help from flash photography. These are different from situations where your flash is the most important light in the room. Concerts, plays, and recitals all tend to have one thing in common: there is a planned lighting scheme designed specifically for the performance. Granted, some of the lighting you'll encounter at a given performance might be minimal or poorly executed, but you'll still have to work with something someone else has put in place as far as lighting goes. Photographing stage performances can be a challenge because the provided lighting does not always show up great in pictures. Hot spots and strange color shifts can leave you wondering why something that looked fine in person looks so bad in your photos.

Here are some tips on getting good shots of bands and other stage performances:

- **Avoid using your flash if you can.** Not only is it distracting to the audience and the performers, sometimes it's not even allowed. Sometimes, you'll find that the available lighting is actually preferable to anything you can do with your on-camera flash.
- **Be aware of the rules.** Check to see if there are any limits to what you can photograph, where you can position yourself and your camera, and how long into the performance you'll be allowed to continue shooting. Even some smaller venues impose a "three-song" limit on photography where photographers must stop shooting and leave the stage area after the first three songs.
- **Use a high ISO.** Most dSLRs are capable of producing good quality images at high ISO settings. If you're not using flash, you'll need a combination of high ISO and wide apertures. If you are using flash, high ISOs will help you get the most out of what the flash can provide at longer distances.

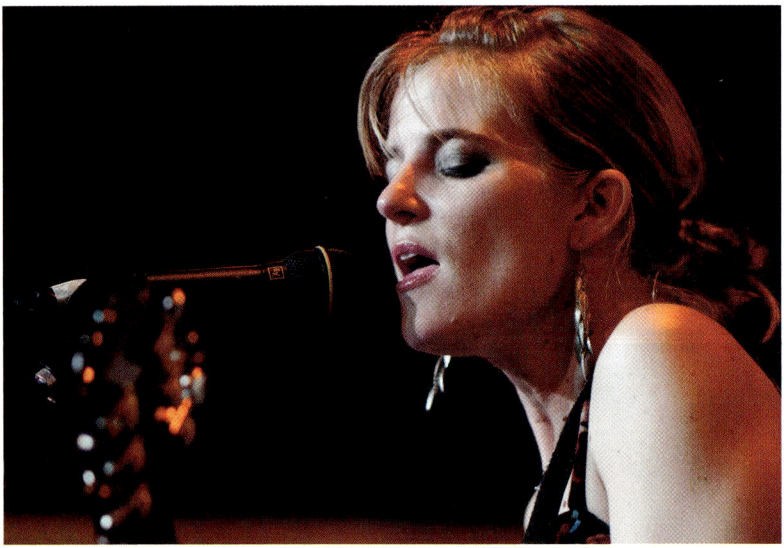

Figure 6.4 If you can make use of the available performance lighting, try shooting some images with fill flash techniques or no flash at all.

- **Watch for motion blur.** If the lighting on the stage is bright and consistent enough for your camera to maintain adequate shutter speeds to prevent blur, then you can use a program mode like Aperture Priority with no problem. In that case, you likely won't need flash at all because the stage lighting will not only be sufficient, but preferable. However, if the stage lighting is very low or non-existent, use your camera's Manual mode so you can control the shutter speed to capture ambient/stage lighting to your liking, similar to how we recommend you shoot any indoor shots.
- **Anticipate the action.** If you're not familiar with the performers' natural movements and style, keep in mind that they'll repeat some of their expressions and body language during their performance. For example, musicians and singers will tend to use the same expressions during similar pieces of music (a chorus). Knowing this will make it easier for you to anticipate a certain look you're trying to capture from the subject.
- **Check the available lighting.** Just prior to the performance, if possible, take some quick test shots to judge the stage lighting and how your flash will appear in the shots.

Weddings and Events

Photographing events, especially weddings, will test your skill with all types of photography. A typical wedding day will require the photographer to capture traditional and non-traditional portraiture, posed and impromptu group shots, still-lifes and details (see Figure 6.5), interiors and exteriors, ceremony (similar to stage and performance photography), candid moments, and many more. It's quite the challenge as everything is moving at a frantic pace, emotions are high, and the action, location, people, and lighting are always changing.

Because a wedding is such an important one-time event, your responsibility as the photographer cannot be taken lightly. You'll be tasked with capturing the entire day in photographs, which will serve as a lasting memory for the couple and their family. Before you assume this kind of responsibility, you should ask yourself if it's both something you can do, and something you want to do. If you feel you are ready and able to take on the challenge, here are some final tips for how you should approach the flash aspect of the photography:

- **Bring lots of batteries.** Make sure you have more than enough batteries on hand for several hundred flash shots, at or below full power, for each flash you'll be using. Invest in quality rechargeable batteries for the best performance, and be sure they are fully charged and ready to go.

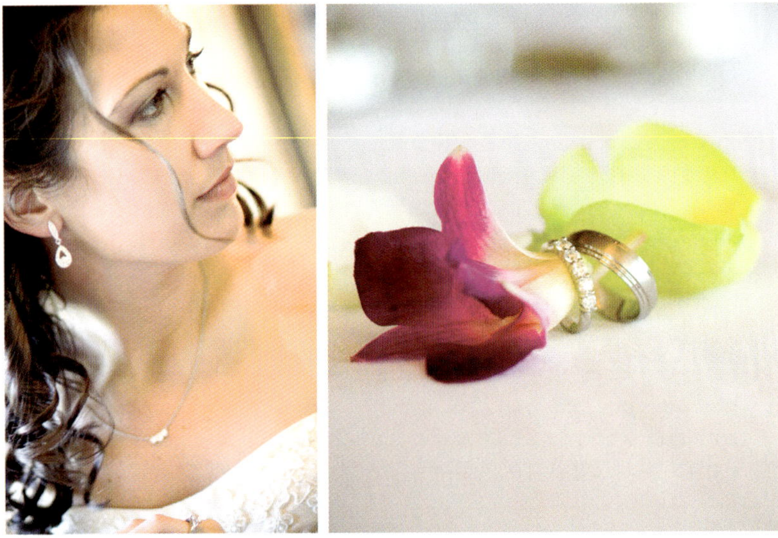

Figure 6.5 Wedding and event photography encompasses many different types of photography and lighting techniques, including portrait and detail pictures.

- **Don't use flash if it's not necessary.** Many of the shots you take can and should be taken without the added illumination of flash lighting. Images of the decor and details, as well as the ceremony can be taken with wide apertures and higher ISO settings.
- **Plan ahead.** Ask for a timeline of the event and determine where you should be, and when, for the pictures you've agreed to take. If you have any questions, discuss them with whoever is in charge to make sure there is time built in to the schedule for the photography you need to do (e.g., formal group photos, portraits, specific shots requested, etc.). Keep in mind, events don't always go according to schedule, and locations for some of the photography may have to change, so be prepared to be flexible with your workflow and lighting setups.
- **Keep it simple.** Use your knowledge of easy but effective lighting techniques to get great shots without complicated lighting setups and camera settings. If you're taking photos in a normal-sized room with good light-colored surfaces/walls, then see if you can get good results with simple bounce flash techniques. You can also get decent flash photos of reception and party shots with a basic bounce card.

- **Set up mini-studios.** Although great shots are possible with the skilled use of on-camera flash, setting up lights off-camera will allow you to achieve more sophisticated looks to your images. Group shots and posed portraits will benefit the most from purposeful setups. For group shots, an easy setup is to place a flash on either side of the group for even lighting. If you find a nice location where you can set up a mini-studio with two or three lights, it will allow you to invite the bride and groom (and/or honored guests) over there for some casual or traditional portraiture.
- **Capture the details and environment, too.** The venue, the décor, the food, flowers, transportation, and all the little visual details that go into the making of a wedding or other event will all be a fading memory unless they are documented with good photos. Instead of flash, use a tripod and long shutter speeds to capture an empty room with good ambient light. If that is not possible, try using bounce flash to light up most of the room in an even manner. Use bounce where possible to capture other elements of the environment, and hand-held off-camera flash for smaller details.

Index

A

B

E

F

L

M

N

O

P

U

V

W

Z